Yorktown: Campaign of Strategic Options

Theodore Thayer

Rutgers University

The America's Alternatives Series
Edited by Harold M. Hyman

Yorktown:

Campaign of

Strategic Options

J. B. Lippincott Company
Philadelphia/New York/Toronto

ISBN 0-397-47335-4
Library of Congress Catalog Card Number 74-31221
Printed in the United States of America

1 3 5 7 9 8 6 4 2

Library of Congress Cataloging in Publication Data

Thayer, Theodore George
    Yorktown, campaign of strategic options.

    (The America's alternatives series)
    Bibliography: p.
    1. United States—History—Revolution, 1775-1783—
Campaigns and battles. 2. Yorktown, Va.—Siege, 1781.
I. Title.
E237.T47   973.3'37   74-31221
ISBN 0-397-47335-4

Contents

Foreword

"When you judge decisions, you have to judge them in the light of what there was available to do it," noted Secretary of State George C. Marshall to the Senate Committees on the Armed Services and Foreign Relations in May 1951.[1] In this spirit, each volume in the "America's Alternatives" series examines the past for insights which History—perhaps only History—is peculiarly fitted to offer. In each volume the author seeks to learn why decision makers in crucial public policy or, more rarely, private choice situations adopted a course and rejected others. Within this context of choices, the author may ask what influence then-existing expert opinion, administrative structures, and budgetary factors exerted in shaping decisions? What weights did constitutions or traditions have? What did men hope for or fear? On what information did they base their decisions? Once a decision was made, how was the decision maker able to enforce it? What attitudes prevailed toward nationality, race, region, religion, or sex, and how did these attitudes modify results?

We freely ask such questions of the events of our time. This "America's Alternatives" volume transfers appropriate versions of such queries to the past.

In examining those elements that were a part of a crucial historical decision, the author has refrained from making judgments based upon attitudes, information, or values that were not current at the time the decision was made. Instead, as much as possible he or she has explored the past in terms of data and prejudices known to persons contemporary to the event.

1. U.S., Senate, Hearings Before the Committees on the Armed Services and the Foreign Relations of the United States, *The Military Situation in the Far East*, 82d Cong., 2d sess., part I, p. 382. Professor Ernest R. May's "Alternatives" volume directed me to this source and quotation.

Nevertheless, the following reconstruction of one of America's major alternative choices speaks implicitly and frequently, explicitly to present concerns.

In form, this volume consists of a narrative and analytical historical essay (Part One), which presents and analyzes the choices which he believes were actually before the decision makers with whom he is concerned.

Part Two of this volume contains, in whole or part, the most appropriate source documents that illustrate the Part One Alternatives. The volume's Part Three offers the user further guidance in the form of a Bibliographic Essay.

With America's bicentennial observations approaching, it is peculiarly appropriate to reflect on a military-political decision situation that, resulting in the 1781 Yorktown surrender by the major British land forces in King George III's unquiet colonies, evoked his acknowledgment of independence. The Yorktown campaign therefore deserves reconsideration. Alternatives open and visible to Washington, other rebel leaders, our French allies, and British military commanders need not have led to Yorktown, or, if there, might have resulted in other conclusions.

Professor Theodore Thayer presents here a perceptive statement and analysis, sustained by appropriate documents, of the perceptions these men had almost two hundred years ago, that helped to make real America's assertion of independence.

Harold M. Hyman
Rice University

Preface

Prior to the campaign that led to the surrender of Cornwallis at Yorktown and the virtual ending of the war of independence, Washington was confronted by two major alternatives for 1781. One alternative which was favored in the beginning was an offensive against New York, the strongest British base in America. The other alternative, which seemed to present more difficulties, was a campaign against Cornwallis's army in Virginia. During the course of events which led to Washington's adoption of a Virginia offensive, many crucial alternatives related to Washington's two major options from time to time confronted the various commanders on both sides on land and sea. Alternatives adopted over the widespread theater of the war reaching into the Carolinas in America and from Europe to the West Indies, led step by step to Washington's decision to abandon a New York campaign and concentrate the allied forces against Cornwallis in Virginia.

For weeks Washington had balanced the advantages and disadvantages of one alternative against the other in an effort to decide whether New York or Virginia should be the target. Finally on August 14, a message from Admiral de Grasse announced that he was sailing for the Chesapeake which, he thought, considering that his stay on the American coast would be brief, presented the greatest possibility for success. Washington could have requested de Grasse to sail for New York after arriving in America, but he saw that the advantages of the Virginia alternative outweighed a New York offensive. The states had failed to provide him with the reinforcements needed for a New York campaign. De Grasse's intention to sail back to the West Indies in six weeks also ruled out a New York offensive. Furthermore Washington had readied himself for a sudden push to Virginia. The stage was now fully set for the great offensive which in eight weeks forced Cornwallis to surrender and convinced leaders in Great Britain that America must be given its independence.

Theodore Thayer
Rutgers University

Part One

Yorktown: Campaign of Strategic Options

1

Washington's Two Alternatives: New York or Virginia

The British Plan: To Conquer The South

On October 19, 1781, General Charles Lord Cornwallis, in command of the British army in Virginia, surrendered to General George Washington and, in effect, ended the long war for American independence. The sequence of events that led to the defeat of Cornwallis at Yorktown comprised a series of dramatic decisions on the part of the American, the British, and the French commanders on both land and sea. Foremost among alternatives that Washington faced was the decision whether to conduct a campaign against Sir Henry Clinton at New York or against Cornwallis in Virginia. The final choice of a Virginia campaign brought about Cornwallis's surrender at Yorktown and the end of the war. The choice was not an easy one; for weeks the final decision was held in the balance as Washington weighed the merits of one against the other.

When the year 1781 began, Washington was far from sanguine as to the final outcome of the war for independence. Help, it was true, had come from France in July 1780, in the form of an expeditionary force of about five thousand troops under Count Jean-Baptiste de Rochambeau. But after six months of inactivity and waiting, neither the expected reinforcements nor a supporting fleet upon which effective operations depended, had appeared.

Washington's army, without money or credit, was on the verge of collapse. "We are at the end of our tether," wrote Washington in April, 1781, "now or never our deliverance must come" (see Document 1). It had been three years since France had made an alliance with the United States, and notwithstanding the encouragements of money having been loaned and a French fleet having operated in American waters in 1778 and 1779, little had been gained since General John Burgoyne surrendered at Saratoga in 1777. In New York, Sir Henry Clinton, in command of the British army in America, believed that if Britain got through 1781 without a major setback, it would be the last year of the war. Discontent was high in America, he thought, and France would not keep an army in America if the war did not end in the current year. There seemed to be nothing wanting to give a mortal blow to rebellion, wrote

Clinton, but proper reinforcements from England and a permanent superiority of the British navy on the North American coast (see Document 2).

While the French army under Count de Rochambeau waited impatiently at Newport, Washington's troops were posted in the Highlands on both sides of the Hudson River near West Point. As throughout the war, his army had suffered through a winter of severe hardships and thinning ranks. In January, 1781, it was plagued by mutiny to an extent that imperiled the existence of the whole army. Like Clinton, Washington felt that the French government was not likely to keep its army in America much longer unless some very effective operations were forthcoming. In Europe there was talk of settling the American war by mediation, a solution as distasteful to Washington as the collapse of American resistance.

Ever since 1778, the British had with marked success concentrated on conquering the South. By commanding the sea, the British were able to transport troops to the South and keep them supplied. Savanah was captured by a British force in December 1778. In September, Count Charles Henri Théodat d'Estaing had arrived off the Georgia coast with a large fleet and four thousand troops to cooperate with Major General Benjamin Lincoln, in command of the American forces in the South, in an attempt to recapture Savanah. A siege was immediately begun. After several weeks of besieging the British, d'Estaing decided that he could not stay much longer. The allies thereupon launched an assault early in October. The attack ended in failure, with over eight hundred casualties for the French and Americans. Among those killed was the gallant Count Casimir Pulaski, who had served as a cavalry officer in the American army. Count d'Estaing, who was wounded in the battle, soon sailed for France and Lincoln withdrew from Georgia.

Resolved upon taking Charleston as the next step in the conquest of the South, Sir Henry Clinton left New York in December, 1779, with an army of seven thousand. He landed near Charleston and with reinforcements from Georgia, soon had the city with its five thousand defenders all but surrounded. By the time the siege began, Clinton's army had been swelled to fourteen thousand by the arrival of reinforcements from New York and the use of the marines. Although Charleston was defended by strong fortifications, resistance soon became impossible. On May 12, 1780, General Lincoln surrendered his army to Clinton. The surrender constituted the biggest single loss suffered by America during the war.

After the fall of Charleston, Clinton returned to New York, leaving Lord Cornwallis with an army of about eight thousand to complete the conquest of the Carolinas. Cornwallis immediately established a number of posts in the interior of South Carolina calculated to cow the rebels and encourage the Loyalists, who were numerous in many sections of the South. But Cornwallis found that the war was not over in the South. Partisans under Thomas Sumter, Francis Marion, Andrew Pickins, and others rose to give him much trouble. To Cornwallis, however, their raids were considered no more than the last gasp of a dying cause.

An American Victory and British Reassessment

More ominous forces, however, soon began to form against Cornwallis. By July, a Continental corps under Major General Horatio Gates had arrived from the North. Upon being reinforced by large numbers of militia, Gates moved against Cornwallis's strong post at Camden, which was held by Lord Rawdon. The latter at once sent word of the impending attack to Cornwallis in Charleston.

Cornwallis marched immediately with reinforcements and reached Camden with Gates only a few miles from the town. The next morning, August 16, 1780, Cornwallis attacked. The result was disaster for Gates and his army. Although the Americans put up a stiff fight in some quarters, they were soon routed and scattered in all directions. Over eight hundred were killed or wounded and a thousand captured. Ten days later, about seven hundred of the vanquished army assembled at Hillsborough, a hundred and fifty miles from the field of battle. Here they were met by General Gates, who had reached the town several days before most of the soldiers arrived.

After the Battle of Camden, the Carolinas seemed to be lost for America. Cornwallis assured Lord George Germain, head of the British war department in London, that "internal commotions and insurrections" would now subside.[1] When the news of the battle of Camden reached England, Lord North was jubilant. The war, at last, he felt would soon be ending. Indeed, nothing after Camden seemed to stand in the way of a triumphant entry into North Carolina, where Cornwallis expected an anthusiastic reception by the Loyalists.

Early in September, Cornwallis started for North Carolina. However, not long after he arrived at Charlotte, he was stunned to hear that his flanking column under Major Patrick Ferguson had been annihilated on October 7, 1780 by backcountry patriots at King's Mountain. Although Cornwallis did not realize the significance of the battle at the time, it proved to be the turning point of the war in the South. Ferguson's defeat was fatal to Cornwallis's plans. For one thing, it intimidated the Loyalists of North Carolina whom Cornwallis had expected to enlist in large numbers in his army. With his force appreciably diminished and with many sick, Cornwallis decided that he would have to return to South Carolina and await reinforcements before anything further could be attempted in North Carolina. He therefore marched to Winnsboro, thirty miles northwest of Camden, and made camp.

Lord Cornwallis, second in command of the British army in America, was recognized at the time Clinton left him in charge of operations in the South as one of the most skillful and enterprising commanders that England had to offer. Born in 1740, Cornwallis was educated at Eton and trained in a military academy in Turin, Italy. At the age of eighteen, he secured a commission in the Grenadier Guards. The following year he purchased a captaincy in the Eighty-Fifth Foot. Six years later, at the age of twenty-six, he became a colonel of the Thirty-Third Regiment of Light Infantry. In the meantime, he had fought with credit at Minden and in other battles on the Continent during the Seven Years' War.

Of a noble family, Cornwallis was honored with an appointment as an aide-de-camp to King George III in 1765. With the death of his father, he inherited an earldom and assumed a seat in the House of Lords. When the great dispute arose between Great Britain and the colonies over taxation and other issues, Cornwallis favored the American position on constitutional questions. However, when hostilities began in 1775, he felt compelled to retain his commission and accept an assignment in America.

With a corps raised in Ireland, Cornwallis sailed early in 1776, to join General Clinton as a major general in an expedition against Charleston, South Carolina. The campaign failed, and both Cornwallis and Clinton arrived at New York in time to participate late in August in the British victory at Long Island. Thereafter, Cornwallis, except for a trip back to England, served as a division commander with the main army down to the capture of Charleston in May 1780.

About the time Ferguson met death and defeat at King's Mountain, Washington took steps to collect and organize a new army for the South. For the assignment, he selected Major General Nathanael Greene, a man equal to the task, if such could be found. For the past three years, Greene as quartermaster general, had made it possible for the Continental army to survive. At the same time, he proved to be Washington's most valuable counselor and aid in one campaign after another.

Only a little younger than Cornwallis, Nathanael Greene's background could hardly have been more dissimilar. The son of a thrifty Quaker who owned an ironworks at Potowomut, Rhode Island, Nathanael gained little formal education. By borrowing and purchasing books he acquired a wide range of knowledge, including mathematics and geometry. When the war began he helped organize a company of volunteers in his neighborhood. Passed over in the election of officers, presumably because of a limp acquired as a youth, he served in the ranks without complaint. Meanwhile he studied military manuals and books on the science of eighteenth-century warfare. Consequently, as a member of the Rhode Island Assembly, he became recognized for his unusual knowledge of military affairs. When the Assembly raised a brigade to go to Massachusetts to help repel the British following the battles of Lexington and Concord, he was selected to lead the corps as brigadier general.

From the time of his first meeting with Washington, the commander in chief entertained a high opinion of the studious but self-educated general from Rhode Island. By the time of the Long Island campaign in 1776, Greene had become recognized in the army and by Congress as the man most likely to succeed Washington should anything happen to him. After Greene took over the floundering quartermaster corps during the winter at Valley Forge, he exhibited his remarkable organizing ability. When General Clinton left Philadelphia on his march through New Jersey to New York, Greene had the army ready to pursue the British. His preparations enabled Washington, "with great facility, to move with the whole army and baggage from Valley Forge in pursuit of the Enemy."[2]

When Greene was selected to command the army in the South, he was no more optimistic than Washington about the future. To Gouverneur Morris he wrote that unless more authority was given to Congress, so that an adequate army could be maintained, the country might as well make terms with Great Britain.

Developing Logistics for the Southern Campaign

Upon accepting his appointment, Greene realized that the military situation in the South was far different from the war in the North. Since the South produced little in the way of manufactured goods, nearly everything, except provisions, had to be brought from the North. Food and forage were available but lack of transportation facilities rendered it difficult to procure them. Manpower was also a problem, for the armed forces in the South were lessened by its swarms of Loyalists and its large Negro population. Organized government in South Carolina and Georgia no longer existed; in North Carolina, it was all but impotent.

On his way south, Greene did what he could to solicit help from the governments of the states through which he passed. In Philadelphia, Governor Joseph Reed procured wagon teams for transporting goods to the South. Governor Thomas Lee in Annapolis and Governor Thomas Jefferson in Virginia promised to do all they could, but were not very optimistic. On his way, however, Greene, who believed in a strong cavalry, was delighted to hear that Washington was sending Light Horse Harry Lee with his legion to add to Lt. Colonel William Washington's cavalry in the South.

As Greene rode southward, he realized more than ever the part played by personal influence in a country where government was weak and in places nonexistent. To Washington he wrote:

"It has been my opinion for a long time that personal influence must supply the defects of civil constitution, but I have never been so fully convinced of it as on this journey. I believe the views and wishes of the great body of the people are entirely with us. But remove the personal influence of a few and they are a lifeless inanimate mass, without direction or spirit to employ the means they possess for their own security."[3]

While riding through the vast stretches of pine barrens in North Carolina, Greene became more impressed with the problems of logistics in the South. There were rivers enough, but they tended to divide the country and make the problems of transportation more difficult. Some sections of the rivers, however, could be used for transportation, and upon arriving at Hillsborough Greene sent out Colonel Thaddeus Kosciuszko, his chief engineer, and other officers to explore their possibilities.

Greene arrived at Charlotte, North Carolina early in December. In this backcountry village of only a few hundred inhabitants, he found the remnant of the southern army. The men were ragged, half-starved, and spiritless; no general was ever confronted with a more depressing sight. Many of the Virginia troops were naked except for breechcloths. All were living in makeshift huts, since they had no tents. Although it looked quite hopeless, Greene set about reconstructing an army. Soon, as Lee said, he turned confusion into order and revived the spirit and will of his men to continue the fight.

Greene was not at Charlotte long before he realized that the region could no longer support an army. Cornwallis, when he was there, had ravaged the country bare, and it would be weeks before supplies could come from other areas. After studying his problems, Greene decided not only to move to a better location but to divide his little army by sending Brigadier General Daniel Morgan into the area near Cornwallis at Winnesboro.

Dividing his army, Greene knew, was a dangerous undertaking. Morgan would be 150 miles from Greene's army at its new location on the Pee Dee River. Splitting the forces left them open to be beaten in detail, since neither division could support the other. But the situation in South Carolina was critical and it appeared necessary to assume great risks. From the region occupied by Morgan, Greene hoped to recruit many soldiers—men such as those who had defeated Ferguson. If they were to turn out and fight the enemy, however, their homes required protection against Loyalists as well as the British. Greene's action, too, reflected his great confidence in Daniel Morgan, who with his riflemen had precipitated Burgoyne's defeat at Saratoga in 1777.

Following the advice of Colonel Kosciuszko, Greene selected the little settlement at Cheraw on the Pee Dee for his camp "of repose." Although the region was not as productive as some, Cheraw was at the head of navigation, and rice could be brought up the river on flatboats from the plantations below. Upon sizing up the situation, Greene felt satisfied. He was far from Cornwallis and fairly safe from attack; he could build his army without constantly being on the alert. However, to lessen the possibility of attack, which was unlikely so long as Morgan remained in the field, Greene foraged the country bare between Cheraw and Camden, sixty miles away in the direction of Winnesboro.

While Greene was establishing himself at Cheraw, Morgan crossed the Broad River above Winnesboro and menaced Ninety-Six and other British posts in the region. Hearing that Loyalists were collected at a place called Hammond's Store House, Morgan sent Colonel Washington forward with his dragoons and about two hundred mounted riflemen. The enemy was surprised and without a loss of a man, Washington killed, wounded, or captured nearly the whole band of more than two hundred Loyalists.

The Victory at Cowpens

Meanwhile, Cornwallis waited impatiently for Major General Alexander Leslie to arrive with reinforcements from Virginia. Upon hearing that Leslie had finally reached Camden, Cornwallis decided that the time was ripe to dispose of Morgan. He therefore detached Lt. Colonel Banastre Tarleton with eleven hundred of his best troops and sent him after the fighting Welshman.

Tarleton, the most dreaded cavalry officer in the British army, approached Morgan's camp at Cowpens on the evening of January 16, 1781. At two o'clock the next morning, he had his division in motion. After a tiring march of eight miles, Tarleton came in sight of Morgan's front line at daybreak. Tarleton never doubted for a moment but that he would demolish Morgan's corps in a matter of minutes. Morgan, however, was confident that his men would prove equal to the test before them. His Maryland and Delaware Continentals and Washington's dragoons were seasoned men inured to battle. Many of the militia, which made up the rest of his force, also had formerly served in the Continental army.

On discovering that Morgan had placed a thin line of riflemen behind trees in front of the militia, Tarleton sent his dragoons racing toward them. But the fire of the backwoodsmen was so deadly that they soon came flying back. Tarleton next directed his infantry to force back the riflemen. When this was done he sent them against the militia who as ordered by Morgan, fired two volleys and then filed off the field and reformed behind the Continentals.

Believing that they had the whole of Morgan's force on the run, the British pressed forward cheering wildly, with bands playing and flags flying. Soon, however, they found themselves facing a solid line of Continentals. After coolly firing several volleys, the Continentals, mistaking an order to extend the line, fell back a few paces. Believing that the day was won, the British came rushing forward like a mob after their foe. Still in line, the Continentals turned about and fired at close range. Then they charged with the bayonet, while the American cavalry closed in on the enemy's flanks. Some of the British stood to fight. Soon, however, panic enveloped the British, and they threw down their arms crying for mercy.

On seeing the plight of his corps, Tarleton tried to charge with the dragoons, but their terror was too great. When Washington's cavalry came galloping toward them, they turned and fled. For a moment it appeared that Tarleton might fight it out with the muscular William Washington, who came racing at him with uplifted saber. As Washington drew near, however, Tarleton fired his pistol, wounding Washington's horse. Then, giving spurs to his mount, Tarleton went racing after his fleeing dragoons.

Morgan's victory at Cowpens on January 17, 1781, was as complete as the victory at King's Mountain, and no less important. Only about one hundred and fifty of Tarleton's men escaped from the field of battle. Seven hundred were taken prisoners while about three hundred were killed or wounded. Against this toll, Morgan suffered only about seventy casualties.

Notes

1. B.F. Stevens, ed., *The Campaign in Virginia, 1781: An Exact Reprint of Six Rare Pamphlets in the Clinton-Cornwallis Controversy*, 2 vols. (London, 1888), vol. 1, pp. 249-256.

2. William Gordon, *History of the Rise, Progress and Establishment of the Independence of the United States of America*, 3 vols. (New York: Hodge, Allen and Campbell, 1787), vol. 2, p. 368.

3. George Washington Greene, *Life of Nathanael Greene, Major-General in the Army of the Revolution*, 3 vols. (New York: Hurd and Houghton, 1867-1871), vol. 3, pp. 61-62.

2

Focus on the South

Cornwallis's Attempt at Revenge: Chase Across North Carolina

When Cornwallis, who never doubted for a moment that Tarleton would win in any encounter with Morgan, heard about the Battle of Cowpens, he was speechless. Shock soon gave way to anger; he became determined to avenge his wounded pride by trapping the victorious Morgan before he would get away. After defeating Morgan and recovering the prisoners, Cornwallis planned to march against Greene and destroy his army as he had routed Gates's army at Camden.

Cornwallis lost two precious days by waiting for Leslie to arrive, and collecting survivors from Cowpens. Meanwhile, Morgan got over the Broad River and was on the road to Charlotte before the British could block his way. This initial failure, however, made Cornwallis all the more determined to catch up with Morgan and destroy his corps. At the Little Catawba, to speed his march, he burned all but his most essential baggage. The emptied wagons were also burned to free the horses for mounting his troops. Taking turns with two men on a horse, his army made great speed but still could not overtake the fleeing Americans. Like their foe, the British were now without tents and largely dependent on a daily collection of provisions. As events proved, when Cornwallis discovered that Morgan could not be overtaken, he should have stopped the pursuit. But finding that Greene's division was marching parallel to his own in an effort to join Morgan, he decided to head it off and force a battle.

As soon as Greene heard that Morgan was fleeing from the enemy after his astonishing victory at Cowpens, he ordered his army to march toward Salisbury, North Carolina, in the direction of Morgan's corps. The two forces, however were not joined until February 8, when they reached Guilford Courthouse farther to the north. At the Yadkin River, beyond Salisbury, Cornwallis nearly caught up with Greene's division as it was crossing the river. But Greene had boats waiting at the ferry, and by the time Cornwallis arrived at the Yadkin all of Greene's army and its stores were over the river.

Finding it impossible to cross the swollen river, in his anger Cornwallis order his artillery to bombard the Americans on the opposite shore. Protected by a ridge, however, the Americans were more amused than frightened by the thunderous fire from the British cannon. Soon the British gunners sighted a house more conspicuous than the others and began firing at it. It was the house where Greene had established his headquarters. Although the roof was hit, Greene kept on writing his dispatches. "His pen," wrote an observer, "never rested but when a new visitor arrived, and then the answer was given with calmness and precision, and the pen immediately resumed."[1]

Although frustrated again at the Yadkin, Cornwallis was no less determined to catch his wily foe. Believing that Greene could not cross the Dan River at the ferries, Cornwallis marched up the Yadkin to the Shallow Ford in the hope of cutting off Greene's escape at the upper fords of the Dan.

Still fraught with disaster, at Guilford Courthouse where he met Morgan's corps, Greene sent Colonel Otho H. Williams with 700 select troops toward the upper fords of the Dan. Cornwallis, he correctly thought, would take the bait and follow Williams. Meanwhile the main army would get a good start for Irwin's Ferry lower down on the Dan.

In addition to the fact that boats awaited him at Irwin's Ferry, Greene had other reasons for choosing this route. Benedict Arnold, then a major general in the British army, was in Virginia with a division, and by taking the route to Irwin's Ferry he could more effectively block any attempt of Arnold's to join Cornwallis. Furthermore, the route lay in the direction of the populous section of Virginia from which reinforcements could come to Greene.

Colonel Williams started for the upper fords of the Dan with Cornwallis following. In a few days, Williams turned aside and headed for Irwin's Ferry, which he reached only a few hours after Greene had crossed the river. During his march, Williams had often been in sight of Cornwallis's van. As Henry Lee afterwards wrote, "The demeanor of the hostile troops became as pacific in appearance, that a spectator would have been led to consider them members of the same army."[2] Bringing up the rear of Williams's corps, Lee and William Washington arrived at the Dan with the enemy in hot pursuit. Leaping into the waiting boats, they made off to the opposite shore with their horses swimming at their sides. The last had barely left the shore before British dragoons came dashing up with drawn sabers.

On approaching Virginia, where Greene could be provided with reinforcements and supplies, Cornwallis at last realized that he could go no further. He was far from his source of supplies and his army had shrunk by sickness to no more than two thousand effective men. Furthermore, but few Loyalists whom he had counted upon had joined him.

To enlist Loyalists and await those coming to join his army, Cornwallis retired to Hillsborough, about thirty miles south of Irwin's Ferry. Upon reaching Hillsborough, he was encouraged by enlisting seven companies of Loyalists. But on the day after Cornwallis left Hillsborough and headed for Guilford Courthouse, an event occurred that brought Cornwallis's recruiting in North Carolina to a standstill. Lee and Andrew Pickens, while scouting for Tarleton, discovered Colonel John Pyle with a corps of three or four hundred Loyalists on his way to join Cornwallis. By leading Pyle to believe that Lee's green-coated Legion was Tarleton's, the Americans were alongside the Loyalists before Pyle realized the mistake. When some shots were fired at Picken's militia, which was following, it was too late for the Loyalists to get away. Instantly Lee's dragoons flew at the helpless foe. In a matter of minutes one hundred were killed and most of the others badly wounded. The news of the annihilation of Pyle's corps almost in sight of Cornwallis's army spread like wildfire throughout North Carolina. Thereafter, very few Loyalists showed up to join the British.

The Battle of Guilford Courthouse: "Victory" for Cornwallis

After Cornwallis withdrew to Hillsborough, Greene recrossed the Dan since large bodies of reinforcements were on the way to join him from Virginia. Soon he was joined by several hundred rough and ready riflemen from the backcountry. Many had served at King's Mountain and were eager to again train their sights on the hated foe. More recruits arrived as Greene maneuvered near the British during the early days of March. Finally, with over four thousand troops, he was ready to court a showdown with Cornwallis.

On March 14, Greene moved toward Guilford Courthouse while Cornwallis sent back his baggage and prepared for battle. So anxious was Cornwallis for victory that he marched his troops eight miles the next morning without breakfast. When confronted by his Regulars, Greene's motley army, he believed, would crumble as Gate's had at Camden.

Greene's battle formation and choice of ground at the crest of a long rise appear to have been flawless. Tarleton, who wrote a history of the war, declared that Greene's position was well chosen "and the manner of forming his troops unexceptionable." His offering to give battle at this time showed good judgment, Tarleton declared. "A defeat of the British," he wrote, "would have been attended with the total destruction of Earl Cornwallis' infantry, whilst a victory at this juncture could produce no very decisive consequences against the Americans."[3] This last statement was implicitly qualified: a British victory was not overly significant, providing the Americans were not completely defeated, as they had been at Camden.

Unfortunately for Greene, instead of holding their fire until the enemy was at close range, the North Carolina militia, which was placed in front, fired and ran. Had they performed their duty, Greene maintained that Cornwallis's army would have been completely destroyed before the day ended.

The next unit of Greene's army to come under fire was the Virginia militia. This body stood their ground until finally the pressure became too great. Greene praised the Virginians for holding their ground as long as they did. They had, however, the advantage of being posted in a woods which prevented the enemy from keeping formation and sweeping down on them with the bayonet, as did happen to the North Carolinians posted on the edge of a field.

The most severe fighting occurred when the British finally were locked in battle with the Continentals. Against the line of Continentals, the British charged with the bayonet. Unlike the North Carolina militia, however, the Continentals waited, and at thirty paces let loose a withering blast that stopped the enemy in their tracks. If the Americans had followed with a bayonet charge as Morgan did at Cowpens, the British army might have been destroyed. But believing he would be risking his entire army and the loss of the South, Greene withheld. Eventually the British gained on the Americans, and Greene decided to draw back and discontinue the battle. If he had known how much the enemy had suffered, he probably would have fought on. The result could have been the total destruction of Cornwallis's army (see Document 2-b).

Next to Yorktown, Cornwallis's "victory" at Guilford Courthouse was his greatest disaster. Of an army consisting of no more than two thousand, nearly one hundred were killed and four hundred wounded.[4] With but a skeleton of an army remaining, Cornwallis soon took the road to Wilmington, the first lap of his fateful journey to Yorktown.

Having announced the battle as a great victory, Cornwallis expected the Loyalists would come flocking in to join his army. Three days after the battle, he issued a proclamation declaring that his victory over the rebels was complete. All the insurgents, the paper read, who would turn in their arms would be pardoned and allowed to return home.

Cornwallis soon found that the rebels were not seeking his pardon and that few Loyalists were any more willing to join his forces than before. "Many of the Inhabitants," he wrote, "rode into Camp, shook me by the hand, said they were glad to see us, and to hear that we had beat Greene, and then rode home again, for I could not get 100 men in all the Regular Country, to stay with us, even as Militia."[5]

Hoping to find much-needed food and forage as well as more cooperative inhabitants, Cornwallis marched to Cross Creek, a settlement of Scotch men noted for their loyalism. But he found that forage and provisions were scarce there, and the men no more inclined to join his army than at the other towns.

From Cross Creek, Cornwallis could have gone either to Camden or Wilmington. He decided that the road to Wilmington presented fewer problems and was not as dangerous at the one to Camden. The want of forage and subsistance on the way to Camden, the difficulty of crossing the Pee Dee, and the danger of being hemmed in between the rivers by Greene, were all given as his reasons for not going to Camden.

When Clinton heard of Cornwallis's decision to march to Wilmington instead of Camden, he was dumbfounded. Cornwallis, he declared, should have marched from Cross Creek to the Pee Dee where, if necessary, General Lord Francis Rawdon could have met him with troops from the garrison at Camden. By not doing this, Cornwallis was guilty, he said, of endangering the whole of South Carolina to being swept by Greene.

After Cornwallis left Guilford Courthouse, Greene pursued him for a while. But like Cornwallis during the race across North Carolina, he was unable to catch up with his enemy. Greene's progress was slowed by having to stop and wait for provisions, since Cornwallis had swept the country bare. Finally, Greene decided it was impossible to overtake the British. He therefore marched for Camden in the hope that with Cornwallis gone, South Carolina could soon be recovered.

Cornwallis's Strategy: March to Virginia

Cornwallis arrived at Wilmington on April 2. From here it was possible to reach Charleston by transports. The idea, however, of returning to Charleston seemed humiliating to him. Furthermore, he had come to the conclusion that a march to Virginia to join Major General William Phillips, who had succeeded Arnold in command, held out far greater possibilities. Cornwallis explained his strategy to Clinton in a letter of April 10. It read in part: "I cannot help expressing my wishes, that the Chesapeake may become the Seat of War (if necessary) at the expense of abandoning New York; until Virginia is in a manner subdued our hold of the Carolinas must be difficult, if not precarious."[6]

A few days later, Cornwallis wrote to Germain. By this time he had heard about the situation in South Carolina, and the news was not good. Greene was nearing Camden and could be expected to attack at any time. However, notwithstanding the threat to Rawdon, Cornwallis declared that it was impossible for him to provide assistance. Furthermore, he pointed out that with an army in South Carolina far larger than his own, Rawdon should be able to cope with Greene. Cornwallis thereupon made a fateful pronouncement. "I have therefore" he wrote, "resolved to take advantage of General Greene's having left the back part of Virginia open, and march immediately into that province, to attempt a junction with General Phillips." This move, he thought, might cause Greene to abandon South Carolina and march back for Virginia where the contest between the two could be renewed (see Document 2-c). A copy of this letter was sent to Clinton in New York.

Virginia had first been invaded during the previous autumn when General Leslie was sent there as a diversion in favor of Cornwallis in South Carolina. When Leslie was transferred to South Carolina to aid Cornwallis, Benedict Arnold took his place in Virginia in December. Smarting for revenge against his countrymen, Arnold landed at Portsmouth with sixteen hundred troops, including a corps of dragoons under the daring and courageous Lt. Colonel John Graves Simcoe.

Arnold had not been at Portsmouth more than two days before he pushed into the interior with little opposition from the Virginia militia. Soon Richmond was taken. Everywhere in his path, military stores as well as tobacco were seized or destroyed. Having accomplished his mission, Arnold fell back to Portsmouth as ordered, to establish a base for more extensive operations in Virginia.

Sensing the possibility of trapping the hated Arnold, whom Americans were itching to hang, Washington urged Admiral Chevalier Destouches, now in command of the French fleet at Newport, to send some ships to the Chesapeake Bay to cooperate with the Marquis de Lafayette, who was on his way to Virginia from the Hudson River with a corps of Continentals. Destouches responded by sending a few ships to Cape Henry under Captain Le Gardeur de Tilly. Upon entering the Chesapeake, de Tilly found that the British had taken their ships up the Elizabeth River where it was too shallow for the French to follow. He did, however, capture a British frigate before returning to Newport. While in the Chesapeake, de Tilly had no communication with Lafayette, who was still on his march to Virginia.

A few weeks later Destouches was persuaded to try again to trap Arnold in Virginia. This time, he sailed himself with his eight ships of the line. However, near the capes of Virginia, he met Vice Admiral Marriott Arbuthnot who had outsailed the French from Gardiner's Island with an equal number of ships. In the sea battle which followed, Destouches came off the better, but failed to follow up his advantage by renewing the fight. Instead, he sailed back to Newport, leaving the British in control of the Chesapeake.

While Destouches was on his mission, Washington criticized him in a letter for not having gone to the Chesapeake with his whole fleet when de Tilly was sent out. If he had, Arnold surely would have been taken, wrote Washington. This letter fell into the hands of the British, who published it in James Rivington's New York *Gazette*, much to Washington's embarrassment.

Not long after the sea battle between Destouches and Arbuthnot, General Clinton sent General Phillips with two thousand troops to take command in Virginia. At this time Clinton believed that Cornwallis was making great progress in conquering North Carolina, and he wanted to help him as much as possible by increasing the pressure on Virginia.

It was not long after Arnold reached Virginia in December, that Washington ordered Lafayette to combat the British invasion with twelve hundred Continentals. After de Tilly's failure in February to strike a blow at Arnold, Washington considered recalling Lafayette who had advanced no farther than the Head of the Elk in Maryland. Changing his mind, Washington ordered Lafayette to join the hard-pressed Greene, then on his historic dash through North Carolina.

By the time Lafayette began advancing again, Phillips arrived in Virginia. Perceiving that Clinton intended more extensive operations in Virginia, Washington ordered Lafayette to remain there. Since Lafayette would be very much outnumbered by the British, Washington soon directed Brigadier General Anthony Wayne, who was in Pennsylvania with his division, to march to Virginia and join the Marquis.

Building Forces in Virginia: American and British Preparations

Although nominally under Greene's command in the southern department, the Marquis de Lafayette found himself in what amounted to an independent command in Virginia as a British build-up gained momentum in the state. Lafayette was only nineteen when he came to America in 1777, to volunteer his services to the Continental army. He was the scion of a noble French family; his father had been killed at the Battle of Minden in 1759. His mother and grandfather died a few years later, and Lafayette found himself in possession of a very large fortune. Yearning for a military career, at the age of fourteen he became an officer in a company of musketeers. In 1774, he married Marie Adrienne Francoise, daughter of the Marquis de Noailles, one of the richest and most powerful men in France.

Inspired by the revolutionary ideals in America and seeing an opportunity to aid in humbling France's ancient enemy, Lafayette secured from Silas Deane the promise of a commission in the American army. In June, 1777, he landed at Georgetown and made his way to Philadelphia, where he presented his credentials to Congress. Having had no little trouble with foreign officers sent over by Deane, Congress, although impressed by the Marquis and his high standing among Frenchmen, hesitated to act. Finally it agreed to accept Lafayette's services as a major general without pay and without a command. Shortly afterwards, Lafayette met Washington, whose liking for the young and enthusiastic Frenchman presently ripened into the closest friendship.

Within a few weeks after he joined the army, Lafayette was wounded at Brandywine and did not rejoin the army until shortly before it went into winter quarters at Valley Forge. Anxious for glory, Lafayette persuaded Washington to send him over the Schuylkill River in May in an endeavor to strike a blow at the British in Philadelphia. The raid nearly cost Washington a corps consisting of some of his best soldiers in the Continental army. Just in time, Lafayette discovered he was being surrounded by the enemy. Most of the troops raced for the river and succeeded in escaping by wading waist deep through the raging water. A few months later, during the Monmouth campaign, Washington for a time gave Lafayette the command of the troops in the lead. This time his performance was no better than before. Looking back, it seems incredible that Washington should have placed so much confidence in so young and inexperienced an officer.

Congress granted Lafayette a furlough in October 1778, to go to France to do what he could to get more aid for America. Lafayette's principal accomplishment during his stay was to help convince the ministers that a French expeditionary force should be sent to America. After finding that his offer to lead the army was turned down in favor of the Count de Rochambeau, Lafayette returned to America in April, 1780, and resumed his place in the Continental army. In December he was selected by Washington to join Greene with his corps of Continentals. Before he was fairly started, the British appeared in Virginia, causing Washington to order him to cooperate with the French fleet against Arnold.

Upon joining Arnold at Portsmouth, General Phillips, who was one of the best officers in the British army, spent three weeks improving the defenses of the base. He then sailed up the James River to attack the Virginia militia and destroy enemy goods as Arnold had done. On the way he drove back about one thousand militia commanded by Baron von Steuben and the equally flamboyant John Peter Muhlenberg. At Petersburg, the British destroyed four thousand hogsheads of tobacco along with several vessels in the James River. Farther on, they destroyed three hundred barrels of flour and two thousand more hogsheads of tobacco loaded on more than a dozen ships.

At Manchester, Phillips destroyed twelve hundred hogsheads of tobacco in the very sight of Lafayette, who stood helpless on the other side of the river. Before nightfall, the British destroyed more tobacco, five hundred barrels of flour, a rope-walk, a tannery, and several ships in the river.

Although his drive was successful, Phillips did not care to push farther without reinforcements. Lafayette's corps of Continentals, although numbering but twelve hundred, was rapidly being reinforced by militia in answer to his urgent appeals for help. However, Lafayette was far from optimistic and had no desire to fight more than skirmishes with the enemy. "Were we to fight a battle," he wrote Washington, "I should be cut to pieces, the militia dispersed, and the arms lost. Were I to decline fighting, the country would think itself given up. I am therefore determined to skirmish, but not to engage too far, and particularly to take care against their immense and excellent body of horse, whom the militia fear as they would so many wild beasts."[7] Lafayette, to be sure, had learned much about warfare in America since his earlier campaigns. He had indeed become a very skillful officer.

Phillips fell back to Williamsburg where on May 7, he received word that Cornwallis would soon be joining his corps from North Carolina. Phillips at once ordered his army to return to Petersburg to await the arrival of Cornwallis. While waiting for Cornwallis to arrive, Phillips became ill with a fever and died. Until Cornwallis reached Petersburg, the command again devolved upon Benedict Arnold who had been acting as second in command under Phillips.

While events were preparing the way in Virginia for the final campaign of the war, Washington and General Rochambeau met at Wethersfield, Connecticut to formulate their plans. New York appeared to be the most likely target for the allied forces, but with Cornwallis in Virginia, a southern campaign had become an alternative which Washington constantly was to weigh as events unfolded.

Cornwallis's March to the Interior

After sending a letter to Clinton announcing that he had decided to march to Virginia, Cornwallis left Wilmington on April 25, with fifteen hundred effective troops. After a three-week march, he arrived at Petersburg to find to his grief that Phillips had died.

Cornwallis learned from dispatches that Clinton had proposed a joint attack on Philadelphia from New York and Virginia. Phillips, Clinton had thought, could sail up the Chesapeake and move against Philadelphia from the Head of the Elk, while Clinton came up the Delaware from New York. In April, when this was first proposed, Lafayette had not advanced farther south then Baltimore. Phillips had then answered that he approved of the plan, provided he was reinforced by about two thousand men. Clinton agreed to this, and sent eighteen hundred reinforcements to Virginia, which arrived about the time Cornwallis reached Petersburg.

Cornwallis got a letter off to Clinton on May 26, 1781, directly after reading the dispatches. He voiced strong opposition to a Philadelphia offensive. Without an intention of keeping or burning the city, the expedition, he thought, would be more harm than good. He also admitted that, judging by reports, it did not seem that the British could retain the interior posts in South Carolina. But this was of secondary importance, since Virginia was the key for conquering the South. "I take the liberty of repeating," he wrote, "that if offensive War is intended, Virginia appears to me, to be the only Province, in which it can be carried on, and in which there is a Stake." Although he had now nearly seven thousand troops in Virginia, a larger number would be required in his opinion to undertake solid operations in the state (see Document 2-d).

Clinton, however, had other ideas. He voiced his strong objections to the march to Virginia in a letter to Cornwallis, written about the time the latter reached Petersburg. Had he known it, he would have stopped the move and ordered Cornwallis back to South Carolina where General Rawdon was being pressed on all sides by Greene. Clinton, however, in a maganimous gesture wrote, "But what is done, cannot now be altered: and as your Lordship has thought proper to make this decision, I shall most gladly avail myself of your very able assistance in carrying on such operations as you shall judge best in Virginia, until we are compelled, as I fear we must be, by the climate, to bring them more northward" (see Document 2-e).

Cornwallis was planning to set out immediately to dislodge Lafayette at Richmond and to destroy all the military stores he could find. After that, he would retire to Williamsburg to await instructions from New York. Taking his light troops with him, Cornwallis soon reached Richmond, where he found that Lafayette was retreating on the road to Fredericksburg. Believing that the "boy" could not escape him, Cornwallis pushed forward after the retreating Americans. Lafayette, however, proved as agile as Greene had in North Carolina. After crossing the South Anna, he marched to the Racoon Ford on the Rapidan River, fifty miles north of Richmond. From this position he thought he could either wait for Wayne to join him or retire further, if necessary. Cornwallis, however, had no mind for another "victory" like the one at Guilford Courthouse. He knew Wayne was not far away and that Lafayette was being reinforced by Virginia militia. Therefore, on reaching the South Anna, Cornwallis turned aside to carry destruction against the rich country toward Charlottesville which had been left untouched by Phillips and Arnold.

In order to destroy as much enemy stores as possible, Tarleton and Simcoe were sent ahead with their dragoons. At Charlottesville, Tarleton succeeded in capturing seven members of the Virginia assembly while destroying supplies along the way. At his home at Monticello, Thomas Jefferson was warned of the British advance just in time to make his escape. While Tarleton was terrorizing the countryside, Simcoe raided Point of Fork where he destroyed a large quantity of goods awaiting shipment to Greene's army.

On June 9, while Cornwallis was ravaging the country west of Richmond, General Wayne joined Lafayette with eight hundred Continentals and several hundred militia. Lafayette was also presently reinforced by six hundred hardy riflemen from the backwoods led by Colonel William Campbell, a hero of King's Mountain. Lafayette's army, with its two thousand Continentals and three thousand militia, by this time exceeded Cornwallis's force in numbers, if not in quality.

About the time Wayne joined Lafayette, Cornwallis was planning an attack by Tarleton upon an important depot at Albemarle Old Courthouse, to the west of Point of Fork. Hearing, however, that Lafayette had been joined by Wayne and was marching back toward Richmond, Cornwallis countermanded his order. He would need Tarleton with the army if the enemy came within striking distance. But the wary Frenchman kept his distance and Cornwallis, after three weeks of carrying fire and destruction over a wide area, broke camp on June 15, and headed back toward Richmond.

Cornwallis's retrograde action may seem strange for a general who had raced two hundred miles across North Carolina in an effort to overtake and defeat Nathanael Greene. However, in view of Clinton's instructions to Phillips, he felt obliged to retire to the bay to erect a strong base for the fleet and for future operations in Virginia. That he was thinking about this problem is shown in his letter to Clinton in which he wrote that Yorktown might prove to be the best site for a base. He had too, as he left off his march into the interior, a feeling of satisfaction for what he had accomplished during his first three weeks in Virginia. He was sure that Lafayette would follow him, and that he would soon have an opportunity to defeat the Frenchman's army.

As Cornwallis slowly retired toward the Chesapeake, Lafayette followed, keeping a distance of about twenty miles between his army and the enemy. Three days out of Richmond, on June 23, Cornwallis stopped with the intention of attacking Lafayette. But finding the situation disadvantageous, he changed his mind and continued the march.

Finally on June 26, advance units of Lafayette's army fought a skirmish with Simcoe's Rangers at a place called Spencer's Ordinary. When he was informed of the action, Cornwallis moved to attack, but the Americans precipitously withdrew. At this point, Cornwallis halted for a week to rest his men. It was early July, the weather was hot and humid, and his men were very tired from the long campaign.

By July 6, Cornwallis had reached Williamsburg, where he made preparations for crossing the James River on the way to Portsmouth. As Lafayette approached Williamsburg, he was erroneously informed that the British, with the exception of a rear guard, were over the river. Believing the corps could be taken, Lafayette sent Wayne forward with a large force supported by cavalry.

When Cornwallis heard that the Americans were advancing, he was delighted with the opportunity of inflicting a crippling blow on his enemy. On the opposite shore he cunningly stationed Simcoe's corps to make it appear that the army had crossed the river and that only a rear guard remained. Then he drew his army under the cover of woods and confidently awaited the approach of his foe. In the front of the lines, his pickets and outposts gave way on orders, after firing a few shots to draw the Americans on. In his haste, Wayne never saw that his only route of escape was a narrow passage between swamps and water. Lafayette, upon reconnoitering, was the first to discover that Wayne was falling into a deadly trap.

But before a warning reached him from Lafayette, Wayne himself saw what was happening. Most officers in such a predicament would have ordered a retreat which probably would have ended in a rout. Wayne, however, again lived up to his reputation as "Mad Anthony." With the enemy in front and closing in upon his flanks, he ordered a charge. Caught by surprise, the British halted their advance. At close range both sides poured upon each other a withering fire. Before the smoke of battle had cleared, however, Wayne was gone. His attack, nonetheless, was costly. Twenty-four were killed and nearly one hundred wounded, a tenth of his entire force.

The battle at Green Spring Farm, fought on land once owned by the famous seventeenth-century governor, Sir William Berkeley, was a narrow escape for Wayne and could have caused the destruction of Lafayette's entire army as it advanced to Wayne's support. The Marquis, nonetheless, saw fit to describe the battle as a victory, since Cornwallis soon crossed the James, leaving most of Virginia in the hands of the Americans.

Disputes in the British Command: Virginia or New York?

While on the march to Portsmouth, Cornwallis received more orders and suggestions from Clinton. Since Cornwallis had indicated his opposition to a Philadelphia offensive and would presently conclude his operations in the interior, Clinton requested that most of the troops be immediately sent to New York. "I do not think it advisable," wrote Clinton, "to leave more troops in that unhealthy climate at this season of the year than what is absolutely wanted for a defensive, and desultory water excursions" (see Document 2-f).

Two weeks later, Cornwallis received a most informative letter from Clinton. Admiral Saint-Laurent de Barras's fleet at Rhode Island, he had learned, would go to Boston, and Rochambeau would march to the Hudson to join Washington in an offensive against New York. Admiral Count Francois Joseph Paul de Grasse with a fleet as well as troops, were also expected on the coast sometime in the "hurricane season." Clinton thought de Grasse would steer for Rhode Island when he heard that Cornwallis was fortified at Yorktown, and after being joined by de Barras, would cooperate with Washington and Rochambeau against New York. However, he was not much concerned about de Grasse since he knew that Admiral Rodney was aware of the Frenchman's plans and would follow him from the West Indies. In regard to despatching troops to New York, he hoped Cornwallis could send him three thousand men, for which he was sending transports. But if Cornwallis needed the troops for the time being, he was not obliged to send more than the Seventeenth Regiment of Dragoons (see Document 2-g).

Ever since he had received Cornwallis's letter expressing his negative reaction to a Philadelphia expedition, Clinton had been smarting over his subordinate's failure to agree with him. Finally, on June 28, Clinton sent Cornwallis another letter announcing that he would send General James Robertson against Philadelphia "to seize the stores, etc." Since reinforcements would be needed, he gave Cornwallis a list of the regiments to be sent to New York. The list included the Second Battalion of Light Infantry, two battalions of Anspach, the Forty-Third Regiment, the Sixth or the Eightieth Regiment, the Queen Rangers and whatever artillery could be spared (see Document 2-h).

While at Williamsburg on June 30, Cornwallis sent Clinton a letter describing the success of his expedition into the interior. After explaining his exploits in some detail, he again stated his dislike of a Philadelphia offensive. As for plans regarding a base in Virginia, he thought Yorktown and Gloucester presented the most favorable locations. However, he doubted the propriety of establishing "a sickly defensive post" which would always be exposed to an attack by a French fleet. Furthermore, he did not think he had enough manpower properly to fortify and hold Yorktown and Gloucester and at the same time send Clinton the troops he desired. "Upon viewing York," wrote Cornwallis, "I was clearly of opinion, that it far exceeds our power, consistent with your plans to make safe defensive posts there & at Gloucester . . ." (see Document 3-a).

Clinton received Cornwallis's letter about a week later, and immediately sent a reply. Stung by his subordinate's criticism of establishing a base in Virginia, Clinton scolded Cornwallis for not marching directly to Yorktown rather than retiring to Portsmouth. Lafayette, he feared, would immediately seize and fortify Yorktown as soon as Cornwallis crossed the James River on his way to Portsmouth. Clinton then tried to make it clear to Cornwallis that he did not want to draw any troops from Virginia if it would jeopardize the fortifying and holding of Yorktown and Gloucester. Clinton wrote: "I therefore think proper to mention to your Lordship, that whatever my ideas may have been of the force sufficient to maintain that station, and the corresponding one on the Gloucester side, your Lordship was left the sole judge of that sufficiency to the whole amount of the corps under your immediate orders in Virginia; nor did I mean to draw a single man from you until you had provided for a respectable defensive, . . ." (see Document 3-b).

On the day Clinton penned this letter, Cornwallis received the latter's letter of June 28, listing the regiments to be sent to New York with General Robertson. Cornwallis wrote back that he would have the troops ready to embark as soon as the transports arrived. By this time Cornwallis was very annoyed with the reprimands from Clinton. Having requested his transfer to Charleston, Cornwallis told Clinton that he would keep General Leslie with him so that he could take over the command in Virginia should Clinton approve of his return to Charleston (see Document 3-c).

Upon receiving Cornwallis's letter expressing his disapproval of plans to erect a base for the navy in Virginia, Clinton had a conference with Rear Admiral Thomas Graves, who had initiated the plan and wanted it implemented. As a result of the meeting, Clinton wrote Cornwallis that both he and Graves were "clearly of the opinion that it is absolutely necessary" to have a station for ships of the line in the Chesapeake. As to the force to be employed, Clinton repeated that Cornwallis could keep all the troops in Virginia, if he needed them. It was apparent, however, that he still believed Cornwallis did not need them all and that he expected a large part would be sent to New York. By this time no mention was being made of the Philadelphia offensive. It had in fact been canceled out. Washington and Rochambeau were now threatening New York with their armies and Clinton needed all the troops available for the defense of the city (see Document 3-d).

Ever since Cornwallis arrived in Virginia he had, in response to Clinton's orders, been having his engineers study the various locations in the Chesapeake to locate for a base suitable for the navy. Finally in letters to Graves and Clinton written on July 26 and 27, Cornwallis announced that he and his engineers had decided that Yorktown was the most acceptable. "As it is our unanimous opinion, that Point Comfort will not answer the purpose, I shall immediately seize and fortify the posts of York and Gloucester," he wrote (see Document 3-e).

Clinton did not receive Cornwallis's letter of July 27, announcing that he had definitely decided to fortify Yorktown, until August 11. In answer, Clinton wrote that he hoped Cornwallis had progressed far enough with fortifying the base to make it possible to "embark the troops you can spare me for operation here" (see Document 3-f).

Cornwallis received Clinton's last request for reinforcements for New York on August 16, about the time Washington and Rochambeau were setting out for Virginia and only two weeks before de Grasse entered the Chesapeake. In his answer, Cornwallis made it clear that he needed all the troops available for work on the fortifications, but that he could possibly spare about a thousand. His words were: "but I request that your Excellency will be pleased to decide whether it is more important for your plans that a detachment of a thousand or twelve hundred men, which I think I can spare from every other purpose but that of labour, should be sent to you from hence, or that the whole of the troops here should be employed in expediting the works." None was ever sent (see Document 3-g).

Cornwallis conveyed his army and stores from Portsmouth to Yorktown and Gloucester during the first three weeks of August. By August 22, the works at Gloucester were quite far along and Cornwallis estimated that they would be done in five or six weeks. At Yorktown, however, his engineers had just completed their surveys and mapping out the plans for the fortification. With all the labor he could command from the army and a work force of about two thousand Negroes, it would take at least six weeks before it would be "in a tolerable state of defense" (see Document 3-g).

The British Decision: The Fortification of Yorktown

Yorktown, Cornwallis found, was pleasantly situated on the banks of the York River with the smaller town of Gloucester in view a half-mile across the river. The town contained about sixty houses by the riverside and two hundred on the bluff. Some were very fine buildings. There were also several churches and a brick courthouse. Most of the houses belonged to Whigs who had fled on the approach of the British. As Cornwallis appeared with his transports, several hundred militia garrisoned in the town marched away without firing a shot. Cornwallis selected for his headquarters one of the best houses in town, owned by a Thomas Nelson, who received him cordially. Nelson, over seventy and considered a neutral, was treated by Cornwallis with every mark of respect. After examining the location, Cornwallis concluded that Yorktown, with what works he could erect, was not very defensible.

Until de Grasse appeared in the Chesapeake with his fleet on August 30, work on the fortifications proceeded at a rather leisurely pace with Negroes doing most of the labor. Even after de Grasse appeared, Cornwallis was not very worried. He did not yet know that Washington and Rochambeau were on their way to Virginia and he believed the British fleet would come and defeat de Grasse. However, with the arrival of the French fleet, work on the fortifications at Yorktown was pushed with all possible speed. De Grasse, he knew, had brought troops with him from the West Indies. If Lafayette should launch an attack, Cornwallis wanted to be prepared.

In retrospect, it would appear that during the campaigning which led Cornwallis step by step to Yorktown, Clinton proved to be the better strategist. Indeed, as a strategist, Clinton had a long list of successes to his credit. It was Clinton who mapped out the strategy for General Howe's victory at Long Island in 1776. Clinton's readiness to offer advice often proved irritating, but it was generally well-founded, and Howe recognized his merit. After he became commander in chief following Howe's resignation early in 1778, Clinton conducted a march through New Jersey upon the evacuation of Philadelphia, that excited the admiration of European military critics. On the way, he fought Washington in the Battle of Monmouth and gained time to complete the march to Sandy Hook and get to New York. Clinton won his highest laurels with the capture of Charleston, when General Lincoln surrendered his army of five thousand men.

Clinton rightly maintained that he never approved of Cornwallis's abandoning the Carolinas following the Battle of Guilford Courthouse. His orders for Cornwallis to march to Camden or return to Charleston, however, came too late, since Cornwallis was already on his march to Virginia. After that, Clinton correctly prophesied in a letter to Germain that all the posts in South Carolina outside of Charleston would soon be lost. But after Cornwallis arrived in Virginia, Clinton had to make the most of it.

Clinton's plans for an attack on Philadelphia, which Cornwallis opposed, had merit. Philadelphia had the largest concentration of industry and commerce in the New World and its capture again would be a devastating blow to America. As a diversionary operation it had much more to offer than conquering Virginia as Cornwallis favored.

The decision to fortify Yorktown was Clinton's, prompted by Admiral Graves's insistence upon having a naval base in the Chesapeake. The decision to keep an army of nearly seven thousand in Virginia, however, rests primarily on Cornwallis's shoulders. But to both Cornwallis and Clinton, Yorktown seemed safe enough at the time. They never doubted but that the British navy would maintain control of the North American coast.

Notes

1. George Washington Greene, *Life of Nathanael Greene, Major-General in the Army of the Revolution*, 3 vols. (New York: Hurd & Houghton, 1867-1871), vol. 3, p. 161.

2. Henry Lee, *Memoirs of the War in the Southern Department of the United States* (Philadelphia: Bradford and Inskeep, vol. 1, pp. 289-90.

3. Banastre Tarleton, *History of the Campaign of 1780 and 1781 in the Southern Provinces of North America* (Dublin: Colles, 1787), p. 277.

4. Cornwallis stated that his army at Guilford Courthouse was only 1,560, but these apparently were the Regulars.

5. B.F. Stevens, ed., *The Clinton-Cornwallis Controversy* (London, 1888), vol. 1, pp. 395-99.

6. Ibid.

7. Henry P. Johnston, *The Yorktown Campaign and the Surrender of Cornwallis* (New York: Harper & Brothers, 1881), p. 37.

3

The Alternative: New York or Virginia

Increased Aid from the French

While the war in the South went on, Washington, from his strong positions at Morristown and West Point, kept Sir Henry Clinton generally confined to his base in New York. From the time that General Rochambeau came to America with his army in July 1780, until Cornwallis entered Virginia in May 1781, Washington constantly hoped that he would presently be able to launch an attack on New York which would force Clinton to surrender and would win the war. However, instead of the northern campaign materializing as expected, it was eventually abandoned for the Virginia campaign, which as an alternative became the most likely to succeed.

During the winter of 1780-1781, decisions of the greatest importance for America were made at the court of Versailles in Paris. The two principal actors in these crucial negotiations were Benjamin Franklin, chief of the American diplomatic corps, and the Court de Vergennes, France's minister for foreign affairs. Franklin had been in Paris since 1776, constantly striving to advance the American cause at the court of Versailles. His labors to obtain an alliance with France were unavailing until after General John Burgoyne surrendered at Saratoga in October 1777. After the alliance was signed in February 1778, France poured money and military stores to America for Washington's hard-pressed army. At times, too, it had a fleet in American waters. Finally, in 1780, France sent the expeditionary force under Rochambeau to America. Even with all this aid, the American cause, as has been related, seemed desperate when the year 1781 dawned.

Franklin's efforts to get the help needed to save America from disaster were enhanced by Vergennes's appointment of Marquis de Segur as minister of war, and the Marquis de Castries as minister of marine. Both men favored giving America as much help as possible in an effort to win the war in one more campaign. However, Franklin was not so fortunate in having the young and flamboyant Colonel John Laurens sent over by Congress to help get aid from the French. Laurens annoyed Franklin by his impetuousness and irritated Vergennes, who had had enough of high-pressure Americans when John Adams was in Paris. In the end, Franklin's persuasiveness and the desire of the French not to see America defeated brought the negotiations to a successful conclusion. France could not loan America the twenty-five million livres Franklin had requested, but it would give outright a gift of six million. In addition, it would send a powerful fleet to the West Indies, part of which could sail to the American coast to aid Washington and Rochambeau.

Although Vergennes was staking much in an all-out effort to bring victory in America, he did not shun altogether the peace proposals which were being suggested by Russia and Austria. France was burdened with debts and its military reverses had been staggering. He realized that a peace such as was being suggested, which would allow Great Britain to keep what it had won, would be calamitous for America. But there might be no other solution, thought Vergennes.

In March, when the final arrangements were being made to send a French fleet to America, Austria and Russia made another move to settle the American war by mediation. When John Adams heard of it, he hurried from Holland to Paris where he voiced vigorous protests against mediation. Vergennes, whose dislike for Adams had steadily increased, tried unsuccessfully to have Congress recall the dour New Englander. In the end, George III turned down mediation and brought the matter to a close.

The French fleet assigned for duty in American waters was placed under the command of the Count de Grasse. At the age of fifty-nine, de Grasse was gaining his first independent command, having been recently promoted to lieutenant general, a rank equivalent to rear admiral in the British navy. During his career as an officer, de Grasse proved to be a man of mediocre talents. In the Battle of the Capes during the Yorktown campaign, however, he was pitted against Rear Admiral Thomas Graves, who had perhaps even less claim to naval accomplishment. The result of the battle, as much as any other single factor, saved the American Revolution. In the Battle of the Saints, eight months later, de Grasse was disastrously defeated in the West Indies by Admiral Sir George Rodney. During the battle, de Grasse was captured and taken as a prisoner to England. After being exchanged, he was court-martialed on charges of misconduct during the battle. Although acquitted, he never recovered from the disgrace of losing the battle.

De Grasse set sail for the West Indies from Brest on March 22, 1781, with twenty-four ships of the line and a large convoy of merchantmen. After a short passage of thirty-eight days, the fleet arrived at Martinque on April 29. Presently, de Grasse had a brush with a British fleet commanded by Rear Admiral Samuel Hood. The latter soon disengaged and left the French free to provision the French islands, which had been in great distress.

Only about two weeks after de Grasse set sail for the West Indies, Lord George Germain sent a letter from London to General Clinton reporting the sailing. Germain thought that after supplying the West Indies, de Grasse would sail with part of his fleet for the North American coast where he would join the French ships at Newport. However, he assured Clinton that there was little cause for worry since Admiral Rodney would surely follow the French and prevent any injury to the British forces in America. In any event, Clinton became aware of the possibility of finding the French fleet on the American coast at just about the same time as Washington and Rochambeau learned of it.

At Newport, Count de Rochambeau and his army found Rhode Island to be a congenial place, although the inactivity was boring. He knew, however, that he was fortunate in having Newport for a base. The British had held the city since 1776, abandoning it in October 1779, in order to send more troops to the South. In commenting upon the evacuation of Newport, Admiral Rodney declared that it would be counted as one of the greatest mistakes made by the British during the war.

Rochambeau, furthermore, had had good luck in reaching Newport safely. Clinton had tried to persuade Admiral Arbuthnot to station his warships in Narragansett Bay before the French arrived. But the elderly admiral, who alternated between fits of activity and inertia, declared that he did not have ships enough to defend the bay. Admiral de Ternay, who escorted Rochambeau to America, at first steered for Charleston since it was thought they might be able to aid the besieged Americans in the city. However, they learned from a British ship captured off the coast of Virginia that Charleston had fallen and that Clinton had returned to New York. By this time, Admiral Graves had arrived at New York with a squadron that brought the British strength up to ten ships of the line. De Ternay had but eight. However, the British fleet remained at New York and after another week of skirting the coast in dense fog, the French finally reached Newport without mishap.

Although numbering only about five thousand, Rochambeau's army was an elite corps led by talented officers trained in the best military tradition. The senior officers were the Baron Antoine-Charles de Viomenil, his brother the Viscount de Viomenil, and the Chevalier de Chastellux. The latter was a noted author and philosopher who found time during his stay in America to write an interesting journal of his travels. There were also such noted figures as Lafayette's brother-in-law, the Viscount de Noaillas, as well as the Prince de Boglie, and the Count Axel de Fersen of Sweden, who was one of Queen Marie Antoinette's favorites. Among the younger officers was Rochambeau's son, who took a prominent part in the siege of Yorktown. Also conspicuous among the officers was the swashbuckling Duke de Lauzun, who commanded a legion of rugged horsemen and infantry, noted for their size and prowess. Lauzun, besides acquiring the reputation of a great warrior, had become a legend for his escapades involving the fair sex. In America, however, like all the French officers, he was on the best behavior.

Plans and Problems for a New York Offensive

Rochambeau and de Ternay had no sooner arrived at Newport in July 1780, than Washington and his generals began planning an offensive against New York. Admitting that the operation would require a force much larger than the combined strength of the French and American armies, Washington somehow thought that the states, now that the French had arrived, would fill their quotas for the Continental line and send militia flocking to his aid. Not knowing that the French fleet consisted of but eight ships of the line, Washington thought that de Ternay could force his way into the New York harbor while the American and French armies could concentrate in an attack on Manhattan.

Washington's first misgivings about the feasibility of launching a New York offensive arose when he received a letter from Rochambeau relating the strength of de Ternay's fleet. Rochambeau, however, was optimistic. The second division of his army was expected to arrive soon and with it should come enough warships to give the French superiority.

Since Rochambeau and de Ternay needed information on operational details in case a New York offensive proved possible, Washington soon sent Lafayette to Newport. Overly enthusiastic as usual, Lafayette exceeded his instructions and tried to wheedle Rochambeau and de Ternay into committing themselves to an immediate attack on New York. Finally, the young man's persistence rankled the French officers to the point where they wanted to see him gone. De Ternay was adamant: under no conditions, he declared, would he jeopardize the safety of his fleet until it was adequately reinforced.

Lafayette went so far in pushing his views as to write Rochambeau a long letter picturing the calamity that awaited America unless his plans were adopted. Rochambeau's answer revealed his determination to treat all officers in the American army, including his countrymen, with the greatest possible courtesy. "My dear Marquis," replied Rochambeau, "allow an old father to reply to you as a dear son whom he loves and infinitely esteems." He then said that it was pleasing for Lafayette to think that all Frenchmen were invincible. However, their lives should not be sacrificed in unsound military ventures. He, himself, he told Lafayette, had earned the confidence of his soldiers because he never risked their lives unnecessarily.[1]

From Lafayette, Washington soon learned that Rochambeau and de Ternay were not about to be rushed into military operations that might prove embarrassing. Realizing that Lafayette was overstepping his bounds, Washington warned the marquis to be careful to point out to the French all the difficulties of a New York offensive. Obstacles, Washington noted, seemed only to increase Lafayette's zeal. In an effort to throw some cold water on his exuberance, Washington wrote that prospects for an offensive, instead of growing brighter, grew dimmer (see Document 4-a).

Not long after Lafayette left on his mission to Newport, Washington heard that Clinton was planning to attack the French at Newport. Clinton had embarked eight thousand men on transports, and with Arbuthnot's warships was sailing up Long Island Sound. Washington immediately wrote to Rochambeau warning him of the threat and promising to attack New York if possible. The British movement, however, ended as quickly as it had begun, with Clinton and all the troops soon back in New York. Attacking Newport while leaving New York vulnerable had been seen as too great a risk. Arbuthnot, however, presently sailed for the waters off Rhode Island where he anchored for a blockade of Newport.

With Newport blockaded, the question arose as to where the second division of Rochambeau's army should land. Washington suggested Philadelphia, giving as his reason that from that city the corps could march to wherever it was needed. Perhaps he had in mind, too, that a body of troops at Philadelphia would discourage any attempt of the British to take the city by way of the Delaware River. De Ternay, however, preferred Boston, since the division could quickly join Rochambeau from there, and Washington offered no objection.

Early in September 1780, Admiral Rodney arrived at Sandy Hook with ten ships of the line. This was disappointing to Washington but even more so was a report which presently came that the second division was blockaded at Brest by a British fleet. With more military reverses in the offing, France eventually canceled the second division. But it would be months before this was known to Washington and Rochambeau.

During the discussions with Lafayette, Rochambeau and de Ternay voiced their hope that they could soon have a conference with Washington for the purpose of formulating plans. In his reply to Lafayette, Washington wrote: "With respect to the Count's desire of a personal interview with me, you are sensible My Dear Marquis, that there is nothing, I should more ardently desire, than to meet him; but you are also sensible that my presence here is essential to keep our preparations in activity, or even going at all."[2]

After repeated requests from Rochambeau and de Ternay, Washington finally set a date for a meeting on September 20, at Hartford, Connecticut, a town about half way between the French and American camps. On the appointed day the meeting was held in a large house belonging to Jeremiah Wadsworth, the commissary general for the American army. From the outset, Washington and Rochambeau took a liking to each other. Rochambeau, who knew little English, was the ultimate in politeness, and Washington was no less courteous. Since it was agreed when the expeditionary force left for America that Washington would be the commander in chief of both armies, Rochambeau took great pains not to infringe on Washington's prerogatives.

Jean-Baptiste-Donatien de Vimeur, the Count de Rochambeau, was fifty-six when he came to America with the French army. With forty years behind him as a soldier in the king's army, Rochambeau was recognized as a field officer rather than a sycophant who won promotions by court intrigues. Officers in general were inclined to consider him as too gruff and demanding, but the common soldiers looked up to him with adulation. Since he had lived in camp much of the time, the soldiers fondly called him "papa" and felt proud to serve in his army. With a man like this, Washington rightfully felt that their relationship would be a gratifying one.

At the conference it was agreed that if Admiral de Guichen arrived by October 1, with a fleet large enough to secure French superiority, an attempt should be made to gain an entrance to New York Bay. If the fleet was successful in the operation, then the French and American armies would launch an attack upon New York. On the other hand, if de Guichen failed to gain control of New York Bay, it was decided that he should sail south with the French army in an effort to revive American resistance in the southern states. During the meeting, Washington, who harbored premonitions that the second division would never arrive, voiced the opinion that France would find it less expensive to give America money to raise troops than to send them from France. Rochambeau agreed, but sending troops was the way his government preferred to do it. Getting more money, he said, was quite impossible.

The meeting at Hartford came at a time when the clouds were never blacker for America. Cornwallis had but recently practically annihilated the American army under Gates at Camden. At Newport, the French were sealed in by Arbuthnot's blockade, and no one knew if de Guichen would ever arrive to bring relief. But more disheartening than all was the treason of Benedict Arnold, which was being enacted while Washington was gone.

Upon returning to camp, Washington revealed his anguish over Arnold's action. In general orders he wrote: "Treason of the blackest dye was yesterday discovered! General Arnold who commanded at Westpoint, lost to every sentiment of honor, of public obligation, was about to deliver up that important Post into the hands of the enemy."[3]

During the winter, while Washington was struggling with the perennial problems of money, supplies, and recruiting, mutiny struck the Pennsylvania line at Morristown. For days no one knew whether it would spread to the entire army. It did spread to the New Jersey line but stopped there after three of the ringleaders were shot. Meanwhile, the Pennsylvania mutineers were mollified and Wayne resumed the command.

Military Hopes and Uncertainties: Conference at Wethersfield

Black as the picture was during the winter of 1780-1781, there had begun to appear some glimmerings of hope on the military front. First was the report of Ferguson's defeat at King's Mountain in October. This was followed by Tarleton's defeat at the Cowpens. In April the news came of Greene's success in North Carolina. Regarding the Battle of Guilford Courthouse, Washington rightfully prophesied: "I cannot but persuade myself (however the Enemy may have won the glory of maintaining the field of Battle) that Lord Cornwallis will find his efficient force greatly diminished by the Number of killed and wounded, and that being encumbered with the latter, he will experience such embarrassments as to retard and injure essentially all his future movements and operations."[4]

It was early May, 1781, when the news Washington had been hoping for finally came. The report came from Admiral Count de Barras, who arrived at Boston from France accompanied by John Laurens and the Viscount de Rochambeau, son of the commander, who had been sent after the Hartford Conference as a special envoy to the court of Versailles. The news brought from Paris was that a formidable fleet commanded by the Count de Grasse had been sent to the West Indies. The exciting part was, of course, that after reaching the West Indies, de Grasse would come to the North American coast to cooperate with Washington and Rochambeau. Most pleasing also was the knowledge that France was giving the United States six million livres. The ships had arrived at Boston containing large quantities of military stores purchased out of this money for Washington's suffering army. The only disappointing news was that the French government had decided not to send a second division to America.

With the good news, Washington felt more encouraged than he had been since Rochambeau arrived ten months before. Nonetheless, Washington had his misgivings. It was not at all improbable that the French fleet would never get to the American coast. The English had a large fleet in the West Indies commanded by two of the best admirals in the British navy, Sir George Rodney and Sir Samuel Hood. It seemed certain to Washington that there would be a battle in the West Indies, and no one could foresee the outcome.

Upon receiving the dispatches from Paris, Rochambeau asked Washington to set a date for a council of war. Washington set May 21 as the time and Wethersfield, Connecticut, as the place for the meeting. Washington took along his artillery officer, Brigadier General Henry Knox, and Louis Duportail, who could act as an interpreter. Rochambeau was accompanied by the charming Chevalier de Chastellux, who spoke English fluently. De Barras did not attend the meeting out of fear that Arbuthnot might attack Newport while he was gone.

At Wethersfield, Washington and Rochambeau first considered the possibility of having de Barras transport the French army to Virginia where General Phillips had been causing so much destruction. Rochambeau apparently favored this. With Lafayette's army joined by his own, it seemed possible to trap Phillips, which was appealing to the French commander. That Cornwallis was about to join the British forces in Virginia was not known at Wethersfield. Nor was it known that Cornwallis would presently be reinforced from New York and that he would have at his disposal an army of seven thousand in Virginia. The question, however, of using the French army in Virginia was soon dropped. De Barras's fleet was inferior to Arbuthnot's, and it was admitted that he would therefore oppose such a dangerous undertaking.

An overland march of the allied armies to Virginia at this time was also ruled out, especially by Washington, who foresaw all the dangers and pitfalls attending such an operation. "The Season, the difficulty and expense of Land transportation, and the continual waste of men in every attempt to reinforce the Southern States, are almost insuperable objections to marching another detachment from the Army in the North River . . ." Washington wrote to the Chevalier de Luzerne, the French minister at Philadelphia.[5]

Following Washington's line of logic, Rochambeau agreed that the French army should join the Americans on the Hudson for a joint offensive against New York. It would take many more men than they had, but Washington had hopes that the states this time would rise to the occasion, and send the men and supplies needed for a New York offensive. Everything after the armies were assembled rested on the arrival of Admiral de Grasse with the fleet. If all worked out as planned, Washington was confident that New York, the most prized possession of the enemy in America, would fall.

Chastellux thoroughly agreed with Washington that New York held the best possibilities for an offensive. Rochambeau, however, remained skeptical. The French ships of the line generally drew more water than the English. It would be hazardous, therefore, for the French to try to get over the bar at Sandy Hook and into New York Bay. This had been demonstrated in 1778, when Admiral d'Estaing had found it inadvisable to attempt a crossing. At the time, Washington had held high hopes of taking New York with the aid of the French fleet. However, after making his soundings, d'Estaing sailed away. Washington never quite believed that the French admiral could not have gotten over the bar. A more audacious officer, he believed, could have sailed his ships into the harbor at full tide as the British had.

Washington's strategy of launching a New York offensive took into consideration the probability that it would aid the hard-pressed armies in the South. Even if New York was not taken, the pressure on the South would presumably be lessened. If Clinton did not withdraw troops from the South, at least he would not be likely to send any reinforcements to Virginia or to South Carolina.

In any consideration of a Virginia campaign, Washington realized that by the time the troops arrived, Cornwallis could be gone. Until de Grasse occupied the Chesapeake, Cornwallis could escape by sea. Lafayette's success in blocking Cornwallis's path if he tried to march to South Carolina seemed unlikely. That Greene could leave South Carolina and come to Lafayette's aid seemed remote. On the other hand, there was no possibility that Clinton would be gone from New York whenever the allies were prepared to strike. The uncertainties surrounding a New York campaign seemed less than those for Virginia.

At Wethersfield, nonetheless, Washington had made it clear that the alternative of a New York or a Virginia campaign must be continuously weighed. In the end, the one finally adopted must depend upon circumstances as they unfolded. "Should the West India Fleet arrive upon the Coast; the force thus combined may either proceed in the operation against New Yk. or may be directed against the enemy in some other quarter, as circumstances shall dictate," was his final answer to this question at Wethersfield (see Document 4-b).

French Plans: To Wage an Offensive

On returning to Newport after the Wethersfield conference, Rochambeau held a council of war on board the ship *Duke of Burgoyne*. The officers, especially those of the navy, were not very pleased with the decisions reached at Wethersfield. By this time they were fully aware of all the dangers attending an attack on New York. De Barras, who was not governed by Rochambeau's orders to recognize Washington as the commander in chief, absolutely refused to take his fleet to Boston, as had been decided at Wethersfield. Military supplies which would be left at Rhode Island, De Barras maintained, would not be safe from the British, who would in all probability pounce upon Newport as soon as the fleet was gone.

The Duke de Lauzun brought the report of the council of war at Newport to Washington, who received it coldly. However, after thinking it over, Washington wrote a very conciliatory letter to Rochambeau the next day. He still considered Boston to be safer, but that was a matter of opinion. "I would not, however," Washington discreetly wrote, "set up my single judgment against that of so many Gentlemen of experience, more especially as the matter partly depends upon a knowledge of Marine Affairs of which I candidly confess my ignorance" (see Document 4-c). Afterward, in a letter to Chastellux, Washington admitted that he had been carried too far in his fears for the safety of the French fleet at Newport.

While still at Wethersfield, Washington wrote Luzerne explaining the plans adopted at the meeting. Since so much depended upon naval superiority, Washington asked the French minister to write to de Grasse and acquaint him with the military situation in America and the plans afoot for an offensive against the enemy. De Grasse specifically should be requested to sail for Sandy Hook, where he would be joined by de Barras. Together they could blockade New York or force an entrance and defeat Arbuthnot (see Document 4-d). Although Washington did not stress bringing the whole fleet from the West Indies, that was the implication. In a letter to Rochambeau written a little later, he said that he had urged Luzerne to ask de Grasse to sail "with his whole fleet."[6] Luzerne answered Washington by promising to do all in his power to obtain de Grasse's fullest cooperation.

On June 10, when Rochambeau was about to begin his march to join Washington at the Hudson, he received an encouraging letter from de Grasse written soon after his departure from Brest for the West Indies. In the letter, de Grasse stated that he planned to arrive on the North American coast to cooperate with the army sometime about the middle of July. Since he could be in American waters only a few weeks, he asked that everything be in readiness for an offensive. De Grasse's letter is not clear as to whether or not he would bring his entire fleet to the American coast. The letter reads: "His Majesty has entrusted me with the command of the naval force destined for the protection of his possessions in southern America, and those of his allies in North America. The force which I command is sufficient to fulfill the offensive plans, which is in the interest of the Allied powers to execute, that they may secure an honorable peace. If the men-of-war are necessary for fulfilling the projects which you have in view . . . It will not be until the 15th of July, at the soonest, that I shall be on the coast of North America."[7]

Upon receiving the message from de Grasse, Rochambeau wrote to the admiral describing the weakness of the American armies both in the North and in the South. Washington, he said, did not have more than six thousand troops, while Lafayette would have no more than two thousand Continentals after Wayne joined him in Virginia. General Greene had been repulsed at Camden and it was doubtful that he could help Lafayette. The military imbalance, however, would be changed if de Grasse could bring five or six thousand troops and a sizeable sum of money. The allies could then attack the enemy either in Virginia or at New York. An offensive against the latter, wrote Rochambeau, was considered by Washington as the most practicable under present conditions. The letter reflected correctly the decisions made at Wethersfield, but in the last analysis left it to de Grasse to decide whether to sail to Virginia or to Sandy Hook (see Document 4-e).

After writing to de Grasse, Rochambeau acquainted Washington, by a letter of June 12, with what he had written to the admiral. The letter reads: "I have already wrote to the Count de Grasse that your Excellency had desired my marching to the north river to [strengthen or even attack NY] when the circumstances will admit of it. I have Apprized him of the number of the garrison at New York and of the considerable forces which the enemy has sent in Virginy, that the only means which seems practicable, to your Excellency is [a diversion upon New Yk.] which you propose to do as soon as the circumstances will allow of it. I have spoken to him of the Enemy's naval forces and told him that by reason of the constant wind, I thought it would be a great stroke to go to [Chesapeake Bay in which], he can make great things against the naval forces that will be there, and then the wind could bring him [in 2 days before N YK.] that if he could bring us some [moveable Forces, 5 or 6 thousand Men More] would render our expedition much more probable and likewise by bringing us [money from] the [West Indies where] it is said that our [Bills of Exchange are at Par]. I beg your Excellency, if youe any thing to add to this dispatch, to send it to me at Providence because possibly the frigate that carries my Letter may not be gone when your Excellency's answer will arrive."[8] (The words in brackets were written in cypher.)

Washington answered that he was well pleased with Rochambeau's letter to de Grasse. "You cannot in my opinion," he wrote, "too strongly urge the necessity of bringing a *Body of Troops* with him, more especially, as I am very dubious whether our force can be drawn together by the time he proposes to be here." Thinking that perhaps Rochambeau was not giving de Grasse precisely the meaning of the Wethersfield meeting, he reminded him that New York was thought to be the most practicable objective at the time. However, with naval superiority, it had been agreed that Virginia might prove more attractive. Therefore Washington asked him to make this point clear if he still had the letter. "And instead of advising him to run immediately into *Chesapeake*," wrote Washington, "will it not be best to leave him to judge, from the information he may from time to time receive of the situation of the *enemy's Fleet* upon this *Coast*, which will be the most advantageous quarter for him to make his *appearance* in." In conclusion, Washington reminded Rochambeau that Luzerne had been requested to recommend to de Grasse that the fleet should sail directly to Sandy Hook. If it were found on reaching Sandy Hook that the British fleet had gone to the Chesapeake, de Grasse could follow. This advice reached Rochambeau after his letter had been sent to de Grasse (see Document 4-f).

In his *Memoires*, written long after the campaign in America, Rochambeau stated that he told Admiral de Grasse that he considered a Yorktown offensive to be the most practicable.* His letter to the admiral, written on June 11, 1781, however, shows that this was not the case. Rochambeau left the decision of his destination on the coast to de Grasse, as Washington preferred.

Increasing the Strength of the Army

After Virginia was invaded by Benedict Arnold, appeals from its citizens for help became louder as the British intensified their warfare. Until Arnold came, Virginia had for the most part been spared the horrors of war, the battles had been confined to the North and to the Carolinas and Georgia. Believing itself to be fairly safe from invasion, the state had been lulled into a false sense of security. Thomas Jefferson, who had been governor prior to the arrival of Cornwallis, had placed civilian needs and rights before the demands of war. In the Carolinas, Greene fumed at Jefferson's lack of decisiveness. Appeals for cavalry horses had gone unanswered. When the British came, Greene upbraided Virginia for withholding horses, which were falling into the hands of the enemy. The horses had been saved for reaping Virginia's own destruction.

Aroused by the state of affairs in Virginia, Richard Henry Lee, the statesman who had made the motion in Congress for independence in 1776, frantically wrote to Washington and members of Congress. With Cornwallis pushing into the heart of the state and Lafayette too weak to stop him, Lee insisted that Washington should be given dictatorial powers and sent to Virginia with two or three thousand troops.

To Washington, Lee wrote: "Our country is truly, Sir, in a deplorable way, and if relief comes not from you it will probably not come at all."[9] Washington answered Lee that as much as he would like to send more troops immediately to Virginia, it was not in the best interest of the country. He assured Lee, however, that by the pressure being put on Clinton in New York, Virginia could expect relief. If his plans were realized, Lee might soon see most of the British troops withdrawn from Virginia.

When Washington left Wethersfield, he knew that unless he could appreciably increase the size of his army, an all-out offensive against New York would be out of the question. At the Hudson River, his Continentals did not exceed six thousand. Many of the regiments were only partially filled, and few recruits were arriving. Counting Rochambeau's army, as matters stood, he would have no more than eleven thousand men for a New York offensive that required at least double the number at his command. As yet he could not count on troops being brought

---

*On suggesting a Virginia campaign Rochambeau's *Mémoires* reads: "Enfin, je lui presentai, comme mon opinion particulière, une enterprise dans la baie de Chesapeak, contre l'armée du lord Cornwallis, que je croyois plus praticable, et plus inattendue par l'ennemi qui se fioit sur notre eloignement."

from the West Indies. The only recourse was to get more men from the states.

With this in view, Washington wrote a circular letter to the New England states before leaving Wethersfield. Without further delay he asked that all the Continental regiments be brought up to their full establishment. To accomplish this, he hoped the states would take sufficient measures to force the towns to furnish their quotas. In addition to the Continentals, he asked each state to have four hundred militia ready to march on a week's notice. Furthermore, he wanted the states to be prepared to muster into service whatever part of the militia might eventually be needed. In conclusion, Washington stated that he wanted to know as soon as possible how many troops would be raised. If it became apparent that he could not expect to be properly supported, he warned the states that he would have to abandon his plans for a campaign that held the highest hopes for America.

As scheduled, Rochambeau reached the Hudson after a march of nearly three weeks. His army arrived at the time Cornwallis was retiring to Portsmouth before going to Yorktown. The march itself was uneventful, except for the crowds of curious inhabitants who came from miles around to see the French army. Never in their wildest dreams had they imagined such a sight. With colors flying and regimental bands playing, the French troops paraded in their handsome white uniforms faced with the colors of their corps. On horseback or on foot, the officers at the head of their regiments wore uniforms that fairly dazzled the spectators.

By the time the French reached their destination, they gained a reputation for discipline and gallantry unmatched in America during the war. In contrast to the British or the American armies, who ravaged the countryside, the French took nothing they did not buy. Farmers' barnyards were not raided for fowl, and fruit ripening on the trees remained untouched. The troops were told that their reputation depended upon strict obedience to marching orders and since they took pride in their regiments, they obeyed. During the march, the Viscount de Noailes won the admiration of all by walking the whole distance from Providence to the Hudson at the head of the army.

The high esteem earned by the French army in America was partly owing to the example set by the Count de Rochambeau. From the outset, it was his firm purpose to create the best impression possible upon Americans of all ranks and walks of life. Since much depended on maintaining good relations between American and French officers, Rochambeau set the best example by his kindness and courtesy. Washington reciprocated, and their conduct was universally followed. Whether the French ministers in Paris realized it or not, they could not have chosen a better general than Rochambeau to send to a country so different from France. A less discreet man could have ruined the expedition and sent the French army home more hated than the British.

One of the most ingratiating of the Frenchmen was the Chevalier de Chastellux, who made friends with Americans wherever he went. After the meeting at Wethersfield, he even went so far as to write Luzerne accusing Rochambeau of not treating Washington with as much respect as was due him. To Chastellux's dismay the letter was intercepted by the British and immediately sent to Rochambeau with Sir Henry Clinton's compliments. When confronted with the letter, Chastellux blushed and could say only that it was written in a flare of temper. Rochambeau ended the meeting by casting the letter into the fire.

Sir Henry Clinton has been criticized by historians for not attempting to strike the French army when it was strung out in its long march through Connecticut. Clinton, however, understood the hazards of such a move. At New York he had only ten thousand troops to man extensive defenses on Manhattan, Staten Island, and Brooklyn. Washington's army was not far away and waiting for a chance to attack New York, should the city's defenses become sufficiently weakened. For Clinton to divide his army by sending a detachment into Connecticut by way of Long Island Sound would have invited disaster. New York could have been taken and the detachment, with no support, could have been defeated. Clinton was too good a general to take such a risk.

Increased Difficulties with a New York Offensive

With the French army drawing near, Washington sent a detachment of eight hundred men under Major General Benjamin Lincoln against the forts guarding Manhattan near the Harlem River. Simultaneously the Duke de Lauzun, who had arrived ahead of Rochambeau, was directed to cross the Harlem River and attack a corps of Loyalists at Morrisania. Although Washington brought up his main army for support, the attack failed. The British were not caught by surprise, which was essential for success. Soon they had reinforcements on the march and Lincoln and Lauzun were forced to withdraw.

Some time before the French arrived at the Hudson, Washington asked Rochambeau if he thought de Barras would consider sending some of his warships to the Chesapeake. Such a force, he thought, would prevent Cornwallis from reinforcing Clinton, as well as keeping supplies from the British in Virginia. "I barely mentioned this as an Idea which has struck me," Washington wrote.[10] De Barras, as one would suspect, would entertain no thought of dividing his fleet with Arbuthnot hovering menacingly not far from Rhode Island.

Hoping to find points where the enemy's New York defenses appeared vulnerable, Washington and Rochambeau crossed the Hudson into New Jersey on July 19, and rode along the palisades examing the island of Manhattan through their glasses. With them rode an escort of New Jersey troops and persons well acquainted with the land on both sides of the river. After travelling some distance, they returned to camp, having gained a better knowledge of the British defenses and the problems attending an attack on New York (see Document 4-g).

On the day following the reconnoitering, Washington and Rochambeau held a council of war with their top officers at Dobb's Ferry. Rochambeau, becoming more convinced as time passed that a New York offensive posed too many difficulties, offered a series of questions regarding their plans. Washington answered that he still thought an all-out attack on New York should be launched if de Grasse was able to force his way into the harbor when he arrived offshore. A New York offensive would also depend on having enough troops available. If these prerequisites were not realized, then the French fleet should transport the allied forces to Virginia in an effort to take Cornwallis. At the meeting, Washington again suggested that de Barras should immediately send some warships to the Chesapeake. De Barras, however, was no more willing than before to risk dividing his fleet. His obduracy, Washington felt, left the door wide open for Cornwallis's escape. "I am of opinion," he wrote to his son-in-law, John Parke Custis, "that Lord Cornwallis will establish a strong post at Portsmouth, detach part of his force to New York, and go with the residue to So. Carolina."[11]

Following the meeting at Dobb's Ferry, Washington wrote in cypher to de Grasse informing him of the preparations being made to cooperate with his fleet for an attack upon New York. "Your Excellency," Washington assured the admiral, "by being in possession of the Harbor within Sandy Hook, would give facility if not certainty to the operation . . ." A word of caution was raised, however when he added: "But the practicability of gaining the entrance will be with your Excellency to determine, upon your general knowledge of the place, from your own observation upon the spot, and upon the information you will receive from the Pilots who accompany you."

Continuing, Washington wrote: "The second object, in case we should find our force and means incompetent to the first, is the relief of Virginia, or such of the southern States as the enemy may be found in, by transporting the principal part of our force suddenly to that quarter . . ." However, Washington said that he hoped this would not materialize since he flattered himself that "the glory of destroying the British Squadron at New York is reserved for the Kings Fleet under your command, and that of the land Force at the same place for the allied Arms" (see Document 4-h). This letter was sent to David Forman in Monmouth County, New Jersey, who was to deliver it to de Grasse as soon as he arrived offshore. Forman, of course, waited in vain for de Grasse to appear to deliver the letter.

On his return, Washington's messenger to Forman, brought back a disconcerting dispatch. Rather than reporting glad tidings of the arrival of de Grasse, Forman said that Admiral Graves had left Sandy Hook and was sailing south with his entire fleet. Washington instantly concluded that Graves was on his way to get Cornwallis and his troops and bring them to New York. The alarming information was immediately sent to de Barras. The latter, however, proved to be as firm as ever against leaving Newport until there was word from de Grasse. His negative response caused Washington to drop the question, since he did not want to assume responsibility should de Barras meet with misfortune.

Washington's guess that Graves was on his way to Virginia to pick up Cornwallis proved to be wrong. He had only gone to sea in search of enemy shipping. However, to Clinton's chagrin, he left without even letting the general know where he was going. The lack of cooperation between the British army and navy was indeed astonishing. In a letter to Lord Germain, Clinton complained bitterly over the admiral's lack of consideration. He only hoped, he told Germain, that Graves would come back before de Grasse arrived. Otherwise the absence of the fleet would "certainly render our Situation critical in the very reduced State of this Garrison."[12]

A few days after Forman announced that Admiral Graves had sailed southward, Washington became all the more convinced that his object was to bring part of Cornwallis's army to New York. A letter from Lafayette had arrived with the report that Cornwallis was loading troops on transports at Portsmouth. With such news the prospect for a New York offensive seemed to be fading faster every day.

"Our views," Washington wrote to Lafayette on July 30, "must now be turned towards endeavouring to expel them totally from those States [Virginia and South Carolina]." An overland march to Virginia, however, seemed about as impossible as ever. "You are fully acquainted with the almost impracticability of doing this by land," he wrote (see Document 5-a). On August 9, Washington received another letter from Lafayette voicing uncertainity as to Cornwallis's intentions. British troops as well as cavalry, he said, were loaded on thirty-eight transports. They had pilots for going up the bay, but he thought that this was only a decoy.

As he pondered his alternative with the thought that a New York offensive looked less attractive each day, Washington began to take measures for marching, to Virginia, in case all else failed. Several hundred flatboats had been constructed at towns along the Hudson which could be dragged overland for use on the Delaware and the Chesapeake. In addition, some of the heavy ordnance could also be carted to Virginia. With this in mind, he directed General Knox to begin planning for the transfer of his artillery and supplies to the South. In Philadelphia, too, Robert Morris was asked to see about transports on the Delaware and Chesapeake Bay (see Document 5-b).

During these perplexing days of uncertainty, Washington was not the only one who entertained fears that most of Cornwallis's army would be gone before anything could be done to hinder him. Light Horse Harry Lee, writing from the Congaree River in South Carolina in August, told Greene that he did not think Cornwallis would stay in Virginia. Leslie, he thought, would be recalled to New York with his corps, while Cornwallis, with all except a garrison at Portsmouth, would sail for Charleston.

Believing therefore that Rawdon would soon be reinforced, Lee recommended to Greene that they strike the enemy with all the forces at their command before Cornwallis arrived. Whether Greene needed the advice or not, within a few weeks he attacked the British on September 8 at Eutaw Springs. This attack was one of the bloodiest battles of the war. Cornwallis, as Greene feared, was not on his way to South Carolina, but the battle forced the enemy to give up more territory and withdraw to positions near Charleston.

The prospect of giving up altogether the long cherished New York offensive and concentrating on Virginia came a step closer when it was learned on August 11 that Clinton had received a reinforcement of twenty-four hundred Germans recruited from the Rhine. To add to the fading prospects for the New York campaign, on the next day Washington received another disconcerting letter from Lafayette. In it he said that Cornwallis was sailing up the Chesapeake as though going against Baltimore and Philadelphia. For his part, Lafayette was retiring toward Fredericksburg so as to be able to give as much assistance as he could to Maryland and Pennsylvania.

On August 14, just two days after hearing the startling and puzzling report from Lafayette, the long-awaited message from Admiral de Grasse arrived at camp. It came through de Barras at Newport, who had at once forwarded it to Washington and Rochambeau. He was sailing, de Grasse said, with his entire fleet. Moreover, he was bringing a detachment from the garrison at San Domingo amounting to thirty-three hundred troops. This was wonderful, exhilarating news. But the destination of the fleet surprised Washington as much as anything. "The whole," wrote de Grasse, "will be embarked in vessels of war, from twenty-five to twenty-nine in number, which will depart from this colony on the 3rd of August, and proceed directly to the Chesapeake Bay, which place seems to be indicated by yourself, General Washington, M. de la Luzerne, and Count de Barras, as the best point of operation for accomplishing the object proposed" (see Document 5-c).

Some historians have given Rochambeau the credit for the final decision to conduct a Virginia offensive. Others have credited it to de Grasse. Of the two, de Grasse definitely has the better claim. Rochambeau had in reality correctly outlined the plans as adopted at Wethersfield and as carefully as possible had weighed the advantages and disadvantages of conducting an offensive in either sphere. After that, he had suggested that de Grasse should sail to Sandy Hook as had been agreed by Washington and himself. As for de Grasse, he understood the problems attending a New York offensive where his fleet might be of little service. Furthermore, a New York offensive could become a long drawn out affair for which he did not have the time. Virginia, however, had none of the problems facing a New York campaign. De Grasse, in fact, believed that after sealing the entrance to the bay, his forces, when combined with Lafayette's might easily force Cornwallis to surrender before Washington and Rochambeau could arrive.

Notes

1. Thomas J. Fleming, *Beat the Last Drum: The Siege of Yorktown, 1781* (New York: St. Martin's Press, 1963), p. 71; Arnold Whitridge, *Rochambeau: America's Neglected Founding Father* (New York: Macmillan Co., 1965), p. 98.

2. John C. Fitzpatrick, ed., *The Writings of George Washington*, 39 vols. (Washington, D.C.: Government Printing Office, 1931-1944), vol. 19, p. 237.

3. Ibid., vol. 20, p. 95.

4. Ibid., vol. 21, p. 402.

5. Ibid., vol. 22, pp. 103-104.

6. Ibid., pp. 207-209; Harold A. Larrabee, *Decision at the Chesapeake* (London: William Kimber, 1964), p. 153.

7. Larrabee, *Decision at the Chesapeake*, p. 127; Henry P. Johnston, *The Yorktown Campaign and the Surrender of Cornwallis* (New York: Harper & Brothers, 1881), p. 80.

8. Fitzpatrick, ed., *Writings of George Washington*, vol. 22, p. 206n.

9. Oliver P. Chitwood, *Richard Henry Lee: Statesman of the Revolution* (Parsons, W.V.: McClain Printing Co., 1967), p. 153.

10. Fitzpatrick, ed., *Writings of George Washington*, vol. 22, pp. 229-30.

11. Ibid., pp. 413-16.

12. B.F. Stevens, ed., *The Clinton-Cornwallis Controversy* (London, 1888), vol. 2, pp. 91-95.

4

The Decision for a Virginia Campaign

Preparations for Virginia

Admiral de Grasse's scintillating message brought to an abrupt end all thought of a New York campaign. But even if de Grasse had sailed directly to Sandy Hook, Washington no longer believed that a New York campaign was possible. The states had failed to respond to his urgent calls for reinforcements and although de Grasse brought troops with him, the number of men that Washington had would have remained too small for promising a successful attack on so strong a place as New York.

Washington summarized the momentous change of events in his diary. He wrote: "Matters having now come to a crisis and a decisive plan to be determined on, I was obliged, from the shortness of Count de Grasses, promised stay on this Coast, the apparent disinclination in their Naval Officers to force the harbour of New York and the feeble compliance of the States to my requisitions of Men, hitherto, and little prospect of greater exertion in the future, to give up all idea of attacking New York; and instead thereof to remove the French Troops and a detachment from the American Army to the Head of Elk to be transported to Virginia for the purpose of co-operating with the force from the West Indies against the Troops in that State" (see Document 5-d).

After conferring with Rochambeau, Washington wrote to de Grasse on August 17, outlining his plans for a Virginia campaign. If Cornwallis was still in Virginia with his army when the allies arrived to cooperate with the admiral, they would launch a united offensive against the enemy. But if a good part of Cornwallis's army was gone, enough troops would be left in Virginia to force the British to surrender while the main part of the army would go with the fleet against Charleston. Charleston would also be the target, if all the British were gone when Washington arrived (see Document 5-e).

One disconcerting piece of information was found in de Barras's otherwise gratifying news. De Barras announced that he intended soon to leave Newport for a cruise off Newfoundland in search of enemy shipping. This ill-judged plan may have been prompted by chagrin at the thought of serving under de Grasse, who had formerly been his junior in rank. Since he had not received orders directing him to join de Grasse, he was free to do as he pleased with his squadron.

When Washington and Rochambeau read of de Barras's plans, they were shocked at the thought of losing his fleet right at the time that victory was at last in sight. They therefore immediately wrote urgently imploring that he abandon the Newfoundland cruise and instead sail to join de Grasse in the Chesapeake. Admiral Robert Digby was coming to America from England with ships of the line estimated to number as high as ten. A separation of the French naval forces could consequently give the English naval superiority on the American coast. Their appeal met with acquiescence. On receiving de Barras's reply, Washington wrote to de Grasse that de Barras would sail in a few days from Newport and join him in the Chesapeake Bay.

Within ten days after deciding to make Virginia the theater of operations, Washington and Rochambeau had the army and all the supplies and equipment over the Hudson River. Washington's detachment consisted of about twenty-five hundred troops. The rest of the army on the Hudson, numbering about five thousand with militia, were left under General William Heath to guard the Highlands. After crossing the Hudson, one division of the Americans directed its course to Springfield, New Jersey, while the other marched to Chatham. The French troops who followed the Americans over the river marched toward Morristown to the right of Washington's troops. Both armies were delayed for want of a sufficient number of horses for the artillery, and by long lines of wagon trains.

From the start, Washington and Rochambeau kept their destination a profound secret. Officers of the highest rank were as ignorant of the objective as the common soldiers. Even General Knox, one of Washington's most intimate advisors, did not know. To his wife Lucy, he wrote that no one could tell what Washington's plans were for "we don't know it ourselves."[1] One French colonel declared, "We do not know the object of our march, and are in perfect ignorance whether we are going against New York, or whether we are going to Virginia to attack Cornwallis."[2] Bets ran high among all the ranks. Most of the men guessed wrong and thought it would be New York, right up to the time that the army turned south and headed for the Delaware River.

In an effort to deceive Clinton as to his intention, Washington adopted several stratagems. By his direction, the French sent artificers to Chatham to build bake ovens. This was intended to show that they would be in the area for a long time. In addition, about thirty flatboats, each capable of holding forty men, were brought along as further proof that New York was about to be attacked (see Document 5-f).

Although Washington's stratagems appeared to have had the desired effect on the enemy, Clinton suspected that they might well be a trick to deceive him. On August 27, while Washington was at Chatham, Clinton wrote Cornwallis that his enemy might be on the way to Virginia. Three days later, he wrote again to Cornwallis while Washington was still at Chatham. "I do not hear," he wrote, "that he has as yet detached to the southward." If Washington did go south, he assured Cornwallis that he would be reinforced from New York. By this time, Admiral Hood had arrived at Sandy Hook from the West Indies and Clinton knew that de Grasse was approaching. Clinton, however, was as confident as ever that the British navy would be able to cope with the French (see Document 6).

Clinton has been severely berated for not attacking the allied forces when they were crossing the Hudson as well as after they arrived in New Jersey. To support their criticism of Clinton, historians quote officers such as Count William de Deux Ponts, who did not, it would seem, understand or take into consideration Clinton's problems. Deux Ponts declared that "an enemy of any boldness or any skill would have seized an opportunity so possible for him and so embarrassing to use . . . I do not understand the indifference with which General Clinton considers our movements."[3]

Criticisms of Clinton, however, overlook many factors. The crossings were protected by fortifications at Verplanck's Point and Stony Point which made it dangerous for an enemy to attack by land or water. To have sent a detachment to New Jersey similarly would have been a very dangerous undertaking. Any force that Clinton could have landed in New Jersey would have been decidedly inferior to the allied army in numbers and would have been in danger of being cut off and captured. As Clinton wrote, "with my reduced force, any attempt of the sort would have been madness and folly in the extreme."[4]

Clinton remained uncertain of Washington's designs until the allies were past New Brunswick and on the march to Trenton. Up until then there was the possibility, he thought, that they would turn eastward toward Perth Amboy and Staten Island. The latter had been reinforced by Clinton, causing Washington to think for a time that Clinton was preparing for an attack.

About the time that Washington and Rochambeau reached New Jersey, Admiral de Barras sailed from Newport to join de Grasse in the Chesapeake. Before he sailed, Admiral Graves (who had succeeded Arbuthnot in July) was by Clinton's prodding preparing to attack Newport. Graves, however, was delayed and de Barras got safely away.

Three days after leaving New Brunswick, the allies reached Philadelphia, where they proudly paraded through the streets to the sound of music and with flying colors. Little did the cheering inhabitants who lined the streets realize the worries that beset Washington and Rochambeau as the soldiers filed by.

A Shift in Naval Superiority

Would de Grasse get to the Chesapeake or would he be beaten on the way? Would de Barras succeed in joining de Grasse? Would Cornwallis be in Virginia when the army arrived? All these questions and others weighed upon the minds of the commanders. Admiral Graves, they knew, had sailed southward from Sandy Hook while Washington was at Chatham. What would happen when the two powerful fleets met? The success of the campaign, and the outcome of the war, rested upon the answer. Washington showed his anguish in a letter to Lafayette. "By my dear Marquis," he wrote, "I am distressed beyond expression, to know what is become of the Count de Grasse, and for fear the English Fleet, by occupying the Chesapeake . . . should frustrate all our flattering prospects in that quarter" (see Document 7).

At Philadelphia, Robert Morris, the superintendent of finance, raised a sum of money for Washington, who feared his army might mutiny unless the soldiers received some pay. Most of the troops were from New England, New York, and New Jersey and disliked the thought of campaigning in Virginia. A little "doucier," Washington rightly presumed, would cause the soldiers to view their mission in a different light.

Upon arriving at Chester, Pennsylvania, on September 6, Washington was met with exhilarating news. Admiral de Grasse was in the Chesapeake with twenty-eight ships of the line, and thirty-three hundred troops under the command of the Marquis Claude-Marie de Saint-Simon. Washington immediately sent a dispatch to de Grasse congratulating him upon his arrival and requesting him to send transports up the bay for Washington's and Rochambeau's armies.

Admiral de Grasse's success so far had been phenomenal. He had crossed the Atlantic without mishap with twenty-one ships of the line and a convoy of one hundred and fifty merchantmen. In the West Indies he picked up seven more warships. After supplying the hard-pressed French island, he captured the poorly defended English island of Tobago. During his operations, de Grasse had a brush with Admiral Hood. The latter, however, found himself outmatched by the French and withdrew.

By July, 1781, de Grasse was ready to start for the Chesapeake. Leaving Martinique, he first stopped at Haiti where he embarked the thirty-three hundred troops commanded by the Marquis de Saint-Simon. It was from Haiti that de Grasse wrote the letter of July 28, which Washington received on August 14, and which changed the whole course of the campaign.

After leaving Haiti, de Grasse stopped at Havana for the purpose of raising money for Rochambeau and Washington. At Havana, he found the Spanish most generous. Francisco Miranda, the future liberator of Venezuela, then a colonel in the Spanish army, succeeded in raising over a million livres for de Grasse. Even the ladies of Havana, it is said, gave their diamonds and jewelry for the American cause. With Spanish pilots, de Grasse sailed through the little-used Old Bahama Channel, where he was not likely to be seen. On August 30, he reached Cape Henry and entered the Chesapeake without the British at New York knowing that he had arrived.

While Washington and Rochambeau were gathering their forces at the Head of the Elk, Clinton, acting upon Arnold's advice, sent the traitor with seventeen hundred men against New London, Connecticut. It was thought that the diversion might cause Washington to send back some of his troops to combat what might appear like the beginning of a major British offensive in the North.

After savage fighting during which an American garrison was massacred, New London fell. Most of the city was burned and a large quantity of military stores were either taken or destroyed. The New London operation, however, had no effect on Washington.

On arriving in Virginia, Washington invited Rochambeau and Chastellux to his home at Mount Vernon. To the Frenchmen, accustomed to the pretentious mansions of Europe, Washington's home seemed rather humble. However, they greatly admired the setting with the beautiful view of the Potomac. Upon leaving Mount Vernon, Washington was met by a rider with startling news from Lafayette. The English fleet had arrived off the capes of Virginia, and de Grasse had left the bay to meet them.

Realizing that de Grasse might meet with misfortune, Washington gave orders for all boats carrying troops and supplies to wait at Annapolis and Baltimore for further instructions. Manifestly, he did not want to have his army caught by a victorious enemy sailing up the bay. Delays such as this were tormenting to Washington. Every day lost, he knew, gave Cornwallis so much more time to fortify his position or to get away.

Admiral Graves left Sandy Hook for the capes of Virginia with nineteen ships of the line. Although he did not know it, he was pitted against de Grasse's fleet of twenty-eight ships of the line and thirty-six when de Barras arrived. How, it may be asked, did the English allow this to happen?

Having knowledge that de Grasse intended to sail for the North American coast during the summer, Admiral George Rodney, the senior British officer in the Western Hemisphere, for a time considered pursuing the French himself from his station in the West Indies. But he was ailing and needed to go to England for treatment. Besides, he wanted to be in London to claim his share of the immense booty he had captured from the Dutch island of St. Eustatius in February. Hood therefore was ordered to sail for New York with fourteen ships of the line. This fleet, together with Graves's squadron and those that Admiral Digby was bringing from England, would surely, thought Rodney, maintain English supremacy in American waters. Rodney presumed de Grasse would take only part of his fleet from the West Indies, leaving the remainder to convey the merchant ships to France. So confident was Rodney of having enough ships to offset those under de Grasse that he took a ship of the line to England with him.

During the whole course of the war, except for this crucial period and for a time in 1779, Great Britain never lost naval supremacy of the North American coast. However, after Spain entered the war as France's ally in 1779, the combined naval strength of the allies was greater than England's. In addition, Holland added its naval resources to allied power when England declared war on the Dutch in December, 1780. With possessions to defend all over the world, the English navy found itself extended beyond its capacity to protect all parts of the empire. Moreover, in fear that England would be invaded, Lord Sandwich, the secretary of the navy, turned down Germain's pleas for a substantial increase in ships for the fleet in American waters. Admiral Digby was consequently dispatched in August with only three ships of the line.

Beset on all sides, Great Britain's condition became perilous in the summer of 1781. In August, while de Grasse and Hood were sailing for Virginia, Admiral Hyde Parker fought a fierce battle with a Dutch fleet commanded by Admiral John Zoutman on the Dogger Banks of the North Sea. Both fleets suffered severely, but the British forced the Dutch to retire and claimed victory. At Torbay on the English Channel, Admiral George Darby waited with twenty-one ships of the line for an attack by a French and Spanish fleet. The latter, however, turned their attention to blocking the supply route to Gibraltar. But they were outmaneuvered and outfought by twenty ships of the line under Admirals Darby, Digby, and Ross. Gibraltar was relieved and the English breathed easier. It was soon after this that Digby sailed for America.

In London, Lord Sandwich was as convinced as Rodney that England had no cause to fear de Grasse. With Digby's three ships, Sandwich reckoned that the British would have twenty-five or twenty-six ships of the line in American waters.[5] Like Rodney, he thought that de Grasse would sail with only about half his fleet. When joined by de Barras, he would still be outnumbered by Graves.

Sir Samuel Hood reached Sandy Hook at the time Washington was assembling his army in New Jersey after crossing the Hudson. Although he had left the West Indies after de Grasse had sailed, with his copper-bottomed ships he arrived at the Chesapeake five days ahead of the French. After looking into the bay and finding no enemy ships, Hood sailed to Sandy Hook to join Graves.

At New York, Hood found Graves unperturbed by the knowledge that de Grasse was approaching. Prodded by Clinton, he was still engaged in planning an attack on Newport, unaware that de Barras had sailed away to join de Grasse. Until it was decided what to do next, Graves directed Hood to bring his ships into the harbor. Hood protested. There was no time to be lost, he argued, if de Grasse was to be foiled and kept from reaching the Chesapeake. Hood's arguments won out and Graves brought his ships over the bar the next day. It was on August 28, that Graves sailed south with his nineteen ships of the line.

Graves and de Grasse Meet at Sea

Delayed by contrary winds, it was five days before the British sighted Cape Henry at the entrance of Chesapeake Bay on September 5. About eight o'clock in the morning, French lookouts discovered the British fleet on the horizon. De Grasse received the report with delight, believing the fleet to be de Barras with the squadron from Newport. A little later, however, when the size of the fleet was determined, he knew that it was the enemy and not de Barras.

As soon as it was known that an enemy fleet was approaching, de Grasse ordered his ships to sail out of the bay to confront the British. Unfortunately for the French, four ships were up the bay engaged in the landing the troops under Saint-Simon. De Grasse was also handicapped by having nearly one hundred officers and eighteen hundred sailors away from the fleet employed in gathering fresh vegetables.

Instead of sailing out of the bay to meet Graves, de Grasse could have stayed in the Chesapeake where his fleet was all but unassailable. Washington, for one, thought that de Grasse should have done this. De Grasse, however, feared that if he did not go out and give battle, de Barras might be discovered and his squadron destroyed by the swift-sailing British fleet. Having more ships than the enemy, de Grasse was anxious to meet Graves and win a great victory which would make him a hero throughout the world.

Because of a high tide and unfavorable wind, it was noon before de Grasse could get his fleet moving out of the bay. During the maneuvering to get into line there was much confusion, as the glory-seeking captains scrambled to get in the lead for striking the enemy. When the long line of ships finally emerged from the bay, there were wide gaps in the line. The leading squadron, especially, was far advanced from the others. The whole performance of getting out of the bay was no credit to either de Grasse or his captains.

The appearance of the French fleet in broken order presented a golden opportunity for Graves to strike and destroy the French van. But Graves was unequal to the occasion. Lacking imagination and tied to antiquated rules of battle, he believed he had to wait until the whole French line was open to attack. Hood saw the opportunity but was powerless to act. In his notes made the day after the battle, Hood wrote that the enemy's van could have been attacked "with clear advantages" since the force of the whole British fleet could have been brought against it.

It was not until nearly four o'clock that Graves finally found the two fleets in a position that warranted the signal to attack. As the British bore down upon the enemy, they had the advantage of wind as well as the greater maneuverability of their copper-bottomed ships. But Graves did not take proper advantage of either factor. A wide gap still existed between the French van and center, offering the British an opportunity of striking the latter with superior force. Hood estimated that an hour and a half was needlessly given the enemy to close the gap. A British account of the battle declared "that to the astonishment of the whole fleet, the French centre were permitted without molestation to bear down to support their van."[6]

When the British fleet finally closed in on the enemy to give battle, it approached at an oblique angle with the ships in the rear far from the line of battle. Consequently, as the ships of the British van approached the French, they took a heavy beating before they came parallel with the enemy and could deliver their broadsides. One by one, however, the ships of the British van and center became locked with the French in a terrific cannonade. The two largest ships in the battle were de Grasse's flagship, the *Ville de Paris* with its ninety-eight guns and Graves's flagship, *The London*, with the same number of cannons. In reality, ships of the line were nothing less than huge floating fortresses capable at close range of tearing each other to pieces.

While the battle raged, Hood's squadron, except for some long distance firing by the ships in front, never got into action. The failure was due to faulty signaling, whereby Graves had flags for both line ahead and attack flying at the same time. Since the battle began after four o'clock, nightfall put an end to the carnage before all the ships became engaged.

During the battle, ships on both sides suffered severely. Worst hit of all was the British ship *Terrible*, which had to be sunk within a few days. In all, the British had over three hundred casualties against about two hundred by the French. Neither Graves nor de Grasse displayed much ingenuity in the battle. However, since the British presently returned to New York, de Grasse was considered the victor and until his defeat by Rodney the next year, he enjoyed all the laurels of a conquering hero. For his part, Graves, who should have been court-martialed, went on to higher places in the British navy. In the eyes of many, however, Graves was the man more than anyone upon whose shoulders rested the loss of the American colonies.

The British Position: A "Lamentable State"

For several days following the momentous battle that sealed the fate of Cornwallis, the two fleets hovered in sight of each other with neither offering to reengage. Presently the French fleet drifted southward toward the coast of North Carolina and finally lost sight of the British. With the way open to the Chesapeake, Hood advised Graves to get into the bay before the French returned. Graves, however, worried about the condition of his fleet, did nothing. Soon word came that de Grasse had slipped back into the Chesapeake. Perplexed by the outcome, Graves asked Hood for his opinion about what should be done. Sir Samuel's reply was a tart note, which read that he did not know what to say over "the truly lamentable state we have brought ourselves" (see Document 8).

The following day a council of war was held on the *London*. After considering the position of the French fleet in the bay, the damage to their own ships, and the approach of the equinox, it was decided that the best thing to do was to sail for New York for refitting and to await the arrival of Digby. The fleet arrived at Sandy Hook about the time Washington and Rochambeau reached Williamsburg for the Yorktown offensive.

If Graves had followed Hood's advice and sailed for the Chesapeake ahead of the French, he might have caught and destroyed de Barras's squadron. The latter had taken a long roundabout cruise to avoid meeting the British fleet. De Barras finally entered the Chesapeake while Graves and de Grasse were to the south after the battle. When de Grasse entered the Chesapeake on his return from the battle, he found de Barras in the bay waiting for him.

Some historians have argued that if Graves had reached and entered the Chesapeake before de Grasse's return, it would have spelled disaster for the British. De Grasse, they maintained, would have set up a blockade and forced the surrender of the entire British fleet. This, however, seems very unlikely. Although inferior to the French in numbers, Graves's fleet in all probability could have withstood any attempt of the enemy to force a way into the bay. With the whole Chesapeake area open to them for provisions, the British could not have been starved out. De Grasse might have blockaded the Chesapeake for a while. Finding that nothing more could be done, he no doubt soon would have returned to the West Indies. Meanwhile Graves could have rescued Cornwallis, leaving Washington and Rochambeau without a prey, and then could have sailed to the West Indies to hold the French in check.

Notes

1. North Callahan, *Henry Knox: General Washington's General* (New York: A.S. Barnes & Co., 1958), p. 178.

2. Burke Davis, *The Campaign That Won America: The Story of Yorktown* (New York: Dial Press, 1970), p. 21.

3. Ibid., p. 26.

4. B.F. Stevens, ed., *The Clinton Cornwallis Controversy* (London, 1888), vol. 1, p. 17; William B. Willcox, ed., *The American Rebellion: Sir Henry Clinton's Narrative of His Campaigns, 1775-1782* (New Haven, Conn.: Yale University Press, 1954).

5. Hood had fourteen ships, and Graves seven at New York (two were being repaired at the time of the Battle of the Capes); two followed Hood from the West Indies, arriving after sea battle, and three came with Digby.

6. Harold A. Larrabee, *Decision at the Chesapeake*, p. 166.

5

British Miscalculation and American Success: Victory at Yorktown

The Allies Join at Williamsburg

Unaware of what would be the final outcome of the confrontation at sea between de Grasse and Graves, Washington and Rochambeau pushed on to Williamsburg while the army waited for orders. To their great joy, Washington and Rochambeau reached Lafayette's camp on September 14, 1781, to find that de Grasse was back in the bay waiting for the operation against Cornwallis to begin.

Lafayette greeted Washington with his usual outburst of enthusiasm and adulation. The marquis only a month before had asked to be transferred to the North, believing that Virginia would continue to be only a diversion in favor of a New York campaign. Now he found himself in the center of a major campaign that promised to end the war. The thought excited him and, as the man who had fought the British against great odds in Virginia, he well knew that he was destined to play a prominent role in the coming offensive. After hugging Washington with all his might, Lafayette introduced the Marquis Saint-Simon and other officers commanding the troops from Haiti.

From Lafayette, Washington soon learned all that had happened since de Grasse first arrived on August 30. Several days had been spent in landing Saint-Simon's thirty-three hundred troops and their supplies near Williamsburg, not far from where Lafayette's corps was encamped. At the beginning de Grasse made it known that he favored an immediate attack upon Yorktown, which he thought could be taken with the forces at Lafayette's disposal. At the time de Grasse did not know how many ships the English would have when they appeared. De Barras, too, had not arrived. What if the English set up a blockade or attempted to force an entrance into the bay? De Grasse was also worried about whether Washington and Rochambeau would get to Williamsburg in time. As a further inducement for an immediate attack, de Grasse offered Lafayette the use of eighteen hundred of his marines.

Lafayette, notwithstanding his relish for the thought of capturing Cornwallis by himself, refused to start an offensive until Washington arrived.

He knew the price his army would pay if Yorktown was assaulted before the big siege guns arrived. In addition, the troops with Saint-Simon were sickly and weak from the voyage and in no condition to stand battle. De Grasse was also persuaded to wait by the intercessions of Duportail, whom Washington had sent to Lafayette (see Document 9-a).

But waiting for Washington to come had its pitfalls. Cornwallis controlled the York River above Yorktown as well as the peninsula above Gloucester. A quick move up the river would present a path to North Carolina. If Lafayette marched to intercept the British, he might fail to catch up with the enemy or could suffer defeat at the hands of his skillful antagonist.

Fortunately, Cornwallis did not attempt to escape or even to attack Saint-Simon during his landing. Saint-Simon was separated from Lafayette's army by several miles; an attack on the French troops would seem to have been the proper action for any enterprising general. Protected, however, as they were by some of de Grasse's warships, Cornwallis concluded that an attack on the French was impracticable. Presently, the French joined Lafayette when the latter moved forward to a position close to Williamsburg.

Until September 8, when Washington's army was at the Head of the Elk, Cornwallis was unaware that Washington and Rochambeau were marching to Virginia. In a letter to Clinton of that date, he stated that he had enough provisions to last for six weeks. Because his inner works were still very weak, he had taken what he considered to be a strong position outside of Yorktown. Altogether, it would seem, Cornwallis was still not very worried over developments. Clinton had assured him that the fleet would accomplish his rescue if Yorktown became untenable.

One of Lafayette's main problems before Washington arrived was to feed his army, which numberd more than eight thousand after Saint-Simon arrived. His worries, however, were soon absolved by the money that de Grasse had brought from Havana. With cash for supplies and with the help of Virginia's governor, Thomas Nelson, Lafayette's commissionaries presently had enough food for the troops. The provisions, including fresh vegetables, soon revived Saint-Simon's men and restored their health.

Some of Washington's troops marched all the way to Williamsburg from the Hudson. Others found transportation on the Delaware and the Chesapeake. When de Barras entered the Chesapeake, followed by de Grasse, they sent boats to the Head of the Elk to bring down men and supplies. Although the progress of the army was remarkably rapid, it was none too fast to suit Washington. Writing to General Lincoln on September 15, he exclaimed: "Every day we lose now, is comparatively an age, as soon as it's in our power with safety, we ought to take our position near the Enemy." Cornwallis, he added, was rushing the work on his defenses "and every day that is given him ... may cost us many Lives..."[1] It was indeed not until September 25, eleven days after Washington arrived at Williamsburg, that all the troops were on hand and ready to begin the siege of Yorktown.

Four days after his arrival at Williamsburg, and before the army had reached the town, Washington, accompanied by Rochambeau, Chastellux,

Lafayette, Knox, and Duportail, paid a visit to de Grasse on board his flagship, anchored with the fleet at Lynnhaven Bay near the mouth of the Chesapeake. Washington was concerned about de Grasse's pronouncement that he could not stay in American waters longer than October 15. This gave the allies only about three weeks to work the surrender of Cornwallis.

De Grasse, who was several inches over six feet tall, greeted Washington, who was but an inch or so shorter, with an exclamation of how glad he was to see his "dear little general." The salutation instantly caused twitters from all the smiling officers. After the greetings, the men got down to the business at hand. It proved not to be difficult to get de Grasse to promise to stay two weeks longer, although he made it plain that that was the limit. But the French admiral balked when Washington asked him to send some ships up the York River to block the escape of Cornwallis. This, he explained would be too great a risk for his majesty's ships to take. He did, however, agree to provide two thousand of his marines for an all-out attack on Yorktown, but not for regular service with the army. He would also supply some cannon and shot.

Encouraged by de Grasse's generosity, Washington asked if he would leave some of his ships after Cornwallis was taken, for an attack on Wilmington and Charleston. With noticeable irritation, de Grasse replied that this would be impossible. The entire fleet was needed in the West Indies (see Document 9-b).

Due to stormy weather, Washington and his companions did not get back to Williamsburg for several days. On the way he sent de Grasse a letter thanking him for his very cordial reception on the *Ville de Paris*. But Washington had barely returned to his headquarters then he was startled to receive a letter from de Grasse announcing that since it was reported that Admiral Digby would soon arrive at New York from England with from three to ten ships of the line, he felt it necessary to go to sea to oppose the enemy. The note alarmed Washington almost more than anything during the course of the campaign. De Grasse, Washington believed, was secure in the bay, and to go to sea and risk defeat would jeopardize the whole campaign. In his letter, de Grasse had declared that he did not wish to remain an idle spectator in the bay or be bottled up by a British blockade. At sea he could exert the full size of his fleet, which now numbered thirty-six ships of the line. Such a large fleet, he felt, should insure victory even if Digby brought as many as ten ships. Graves would not have more than twenty-eight ships at most, he reckoned.

On receiving de Grasse's alarming letter, Washington at once sent Lafayette with a vigorous protest to the admiral. In the most graphic terms Washington pictured the calamity that de Grasse's departure could cause. "You Excellency's departure from the Chesapeake by affordig an opening for the succor of York, which the enemy [would] instantly avail himself of, would frustrate these brilliant prospects, and the consequence would be not only the disgrace and loss of renouncing an enterprise, upon which the fairest expectations of the Allies have been founded, after the most expensive preparations and uncommon exertions and fatigues; but the disbanding perhaps the whole Army for want of provisions." Skillful mariners, he told de Grasse, had declared that the French fleet could repel any force brought against it in the bay (see Document 9-c).

If Washington's strong protest was not enough, de Grasse found himself opposed by his captains who, in a council of war, voted against leaving the bay. Considering all factors, they concluded that to change plans and go to sea might upset the "aim we had in view." De Grasse bowed gracefully to Washington's appeal and the decision of his captains and announced that the fleet would remain in the Chesapeake. Washington wrote the admiral congratulating him upon his wise decision. The "resolution of your Excellency," wrote Washington, "proves that a great Mind knows how to make personal sacrifices to secure an important general Good."[2] Rochambeau assured de Grasse that he was "the most amiable admiral," he had the pleasure of knowing.

Washington Moves to Yorktown: Cornwallis Waits

Washington had no sooner ironed out his last difficulty with de Grasse than he gave orders for the army to march for Yorktown, ten miles away. On arriving on the outskirts of the town, the army took up positions ringing Yorktown. The line was several miles long, with the Americans to the right and the French to the left. At the same time, General George Weeden with Virginia militia and the Duke de Lauzun with his legion advanced to a position above Gloucester. For all, Washington's order was that if Cornwallis came out to fight, the troops should rely principally upon the bayonet "that they may prove the Vanity of the Boast which the British make of their particular prowess in deciding Battles with that Weapon." He knew the French "whose National Weapon is that of close fight," would do the same (see Document 9-d).

On ordering the march to Yorktown, Washington was none too optimistic that Cornwallis could be forced to surrender before the time given by de Grasse for his departure. From deserters, he heard that with a large store of provisions, it would be a long time before the enemy was starved out. His best hope was that when his heavy artillery was brought into play, the enemy would soon give up. Washington was also concerned about the reports that Digby would have ten ships of the line. The British would then have too many ships not to give uneasiness to a commanding general.

Making camp on the ground chosen by Washington progressed rapidly. Within a few hours there were patches of tents dotting the landscape, and a great bustle of getting settled. Orders were given that no soldiers could visit any of the houses of the neighborhood or borrow tools or utensils from the inhabitants since "our ingenious Enemy" had propagated the smallpox in the area.

As the allies took positions surrounding Yorktown and Gloucester, there was some skirmishing with the enemy. The principal action near Yorktown took place between American riflemen and Hessian Yagers, with the latter suffering the most. Three days after the allies arrived at Yorktown, Cornwallis during the night abandoned his outer works and retired to his fortifications close to the town. Many of his officers strongly objected to the move, since it would cost Washington both time and men in taking the outer lines. Cornwallis, however, thought that he did not have men enough properly to defend the lines, which would be in danger of being punctured and outflanked. In addition, Cornwallis did not know that Washington had the heavy cannon brought from Newport by de Barras. If he had known this, undoubtedly he would have retained his outer lines as long as possible. It proved to be a costly mistake which soon brought about Cornwallis's downfall.

Upon Washington's appearance, Cornwallis wrote a cryptic letter to Clinton on the state of affairs at Yorktown. His army, he confidently wrote, was staring the whole allied force in the face and only wished they would attack. He was retiring to his inner works, he said, with the assurance that if relief came in a reasonable length of time, all would be safe at Yorktown and Gloucester. During the day Cornwallis had received a letter from Clinton that had buoyed his spirits. Admiral Digby had arrived with three ships of the line. Furthermore, Clinton had five thousand troops loaded on transports ready to depart for Virginia on October 5 (see Document 10-a).

Within a week after writing his reassuring letter to Cornwallis, Clinton suddenly became much less optimistic. Admiral Graves now announced that it would be impossible to set sail before the twelfth. It must have been of small comfort to Cornwallis to read that Clinton would come to his rescue if it took to the middle of November. But if Cornwallis found he could not hold out, as a last resort Clinton promised to launch an attack on Philadelphia. This, he thought, might cause Washington to detach some of his troops and afford Cornwallis an opportunity to escape by land. Written on September 30, the latter shows that finally Clinton had awakened to the desperate state of affairs at Yorktown (see Document 10-b).

On viewing the situation after Cornwallis withdrew to his inner lines, Washington thought he was perhaps preparing for a dash to North Carolina. The British still controlled the York River upstream for twenty-five miles and they had a hundred or more large and small ships and boats in the river. By sailing at night, Washington knew that Cornwallis might circle around the allied armies and get a good start for the Carolinas. Thoughts like this were indeed going through Cornwallis's mind. But he still believed Clinton and Graves would come to his rescue. So he waited while the noose grew tighter by the day.

As soon as the British withdrew from their outer lines, the Americans and French advanced and took possession of the works. Men then fell to work strengthening the lines and building redoubts. Meanwhile, other soldiers with horses and oxen were engaged in hauling the heavy cannon from Williamsburg and getting positions ready for the batteries.

Finding that his force at Gloucester was inadequate, Cornwallis sent Colonel Tarleton with his legion to join the garrison, which consisted of

Simcoe's Rangers, some Hessian Yagers, two companies of light infantry, and the North Carolina provincials. Until pressure from the enemy forced them to retire within the confines of Gloucester, these troops foraged the area for every bit of food for man or beast.

Pitted against Tarleton, who was given command at Gloucester, were the six hundred cavalry and infantry with the Duke de Lauzun and about fifteen hundred militia with Brigadier General George Weeden. At first Lauzun erroneously thought that Weeden stayed ten miles from Gloucester because the sound of gunfire unnerved him. This was not the case at all. Weeden had fought valiantly at Brandywine and in other battles with the Continental army. He stayed back, following Washington's orders because the militia had a reputation of being easily routed and he did not want the morale of the army to be shaken at the outset.

Finding it necessary to coordinate the duke's corps and the militia, Washington sent the Marquis Claude Gabriel de Choisy, who had arrived with de Barras, to take command on the Gloucester side. Until then, Washington had not known what to do with the excitable de Choisy, who was not wanted by the officers with Rochambeau. Since de Choisy needed more men to cope with Tarleton and force the British into Gloucester, Washington persuaded de Grasse to send eight hundred marines to the marquis from the fleet.

Early in October, de Choisy ordered his division to advance to a position nearer Gloucester. On the same day the British were out foraging with nearly their whole force. It was not long before the two caught sight of each other and drew up for battle. Lauzun opened the battle by charging fearlessly at Tarleton and his dragoons. In the melee which followed, Tarleton was thrown from his horse but succeeded in mounting another. He was saved only then by the sudden appearance of his main body of cavalry. Finding himself outnumbered, Lauzun fell back to his reserves. Tarleton also soon withdrew on discovering that part of Weeden's militia had come up to support the French. The whole affair was but little more than a skirmish, but Tarleton now knew that de Choisy had become too strong to be attacked without incurring heavy losses. From that time on until the surrender, the British kept within their lines at Gloucester. Finding little to fear from the enemy, de Choisy moved closer to the town and set up a siege.

Victory

On the evening of the sixth of October, nine days after taking the position outside of Yorktown, Washington ordered parallels to be erected for closing in on the British. Positions for two parallels had been staked out by American and French engineers at distances of about a quarter of a mile from the enemy's lines. Between the parallels and the allied camps, especially on the American side, the ground was cut up by numerous ravines which afforded cover for the troops in going and returning from the parallels.

Fifteen hundred troops, commanded by General Lincoln and Baron Vionenil for the French, were selected for digging the parallels, and twenty-eight hundred for guards. All reached the lines defined for the parallels without detection by the enemy, and the diggers fell to work with picks and shovels. The soil was light and the work of digging trenches and piling up the dirt progressed swiftly. The men worked silently and, since the night was dark and cloudy, the British remained entirely unaware of what was happening. With daylight, they saw to their amazement the long line of embankments rising ominously in front of their works. Washington recorded in his diary that "before Morning the Trenches were in such forwardness as to cover the Men from the enemy's fire."[3]

The first corps of Continental troops sent to man the American parallel was a body of light infantry under Lafayette. Each day a new corps was sent to the parallel as the other was withdrawn to recuperate. At the parallels the men were ordered, if attacked, to receive the enemy with the bayonet and not to fire until they were in retreat. During the night the parallels were enlarged and strengthened, while heavy siege cannon were drawn up and placed in position. Washington cautioned his officers to take care that the labor was evenly distributed and that relays should be frequent, so that the work could proceed as fast as possible. All the time the British kept up a heavy fire upon the allied works, but casualties were light.

By the afternoon of October 9, enough batteries had been erected to begin blasting the enemy's lines. The first firing came from the French, who opened with four twelve pounders and some mortars. The firing caused a British war ship anchored at Yorktown to find shelter on the Gloucester side of the river. A few hours later, an American battery began firing from a half-dozen eighteen and twenty-four pounders.

At his headquarters at Thomas Nelson's house, Cornwallis was astounded to find that his enemies were equipped with heavy siege cannon. From his lines soon came ominous reports of heavy casualties and terrific destruction on all sides. Cornwallis now saw fit to abandon the Nelson house and took refuge in a cave in the side of the river bank. On October 11, two days after the allies began cannonading Yorktown, Cornwallis wrote a gloomy letter to Clinton. Only a successful naval action against de Grasse, he said, could save him. Firing from the enemy's batteries had been incessant since it began. Seventy men had been killed or wounded, and the damage to the town and works was enormous. Against such powerful batteries, "we cannot hope to make a very long resistance," he told Clinton.[4]

Two more batteries were opened upon the British on the day following the first ones. The French "Grand Battery" mounted ten eighteen and twenty-four pounders and six mortars. The second American battery had four twenty-four pounders and two mortars. Hot shot from the French batteries soon set fire to three British ships, and all the others had to get out of range as fast as possible. By this time, counting cannons of all sizes, over fifty cannons, howitzers, and mortars were throwing shot and shells into Yorktown so fast that the air resounded with one continuous roar.

With the British already unable to show their heads above their works, Washington ordered a second range of parallels to be erected halfway between the first ones and the enemy's lines. The new parallels were begun on the night of October 11. Unlike the night when the first parallels were begun, this night proved to be full of frightening experiences. The workers were soon discovered by the British, who poured upon the Americans and French all the shot and shells they could muster. Meanwhile, the American and French batteries fired incessantly at the enemy's lines. At times, the troops could do nothing but hug the ground as the cross fire streaked over them. When an enemy's shell fell near Baron von Steuben, he threw himself into a trench. Wayne, who was close by, nearly fell on top of the baron as he dove for shelter before the shell exploded. After a while, the allied guns almost silenced the enemy fire. Soon the dirt was high enough to protect the men fairly well and the work went faster.

It was soon decided that the second parallel on the American side would prove vulnerable unless it was extended to the river. To do this it was necessary first to take two strong British redoubts anchoring the British left wing. It was therefore decided that an assault on both redoubts would be undertaken simultaneously, with the Americans attacking the one near the river and the French the one some distance to the left.

Both assaults proved successful. The French, however, suffered the most casualties with fifteen killed and over seventy wounded. The enemy at this redoubt had eighteen killed and forty-two captured; the rest escaped. Colonel Alexander Hamilton commanded the American corps of four hundred men, selected for their prowess and bravery, who rushed the redoubt near the river. Lieutenant John Mansfield led the way with twenty stouthearted men. Breaking through the obstructions, they scaled the parapet and came jumping down on the defenders in the fort. In the fray, Mansfield was wounded by a bayonet. Colonel Stephen Olney, leading his Rhode Island men, was also severely wounded. However, in a matter of minutes, the British officers in command were seized and resistance collapsed. Some of the British were killed or captured, but most succeeded in making their escape.

Exhilarated by the valor and success in taking the redoubts, Washington praised the men in general orders. To Congress, he reported that the soldiers "advanced under the fire of the Enemy without returning a shot and affected the business with the Bayonet only."[5]

The night after the redoubts were taken, the British made a sortie against the advanced American and French batteries in a vain effort to stop some of the cannonading. Four hundred select troops under Lt. Colonel Robert Abercrombie comprised the daring corps. With fixed bayonets they fell upon the batteries and fought desperately as some of their men drove their bayonets into the touch-holes of the cannons and broke them off. The sortie, however, was repulsed about as quickly as it begun. It was a gallant attempt, but it availed nothing for the British. Within a few hours the spikes were removed from the cannons and they were firing again.

On the day the sortie was made, Cornwallis wrote his last letter to Clinton before he surrendered. With doleful words he told how the allies had carried his redoubts and made them part of the second allied parallel. "My situation," he continued, "now becomes very critical, we dare not show a gun to their old batteries, and I expect that their new ones will open tomorrow morning." In conclusion, he sadly noted, "The safety of the place is, therefore, so precarious, that I cannot recommend that the fleet and army should run great risque in endeavouring to save us" (see Document 10-c).

Cornwallis now tried to do what he should have done weeks before. On the night of the sixteenth, following another day of nerve-rending bombarding by the allies, he frantically began loading his troops on boats. If he could get his army over the river to Gloucester, he planned to march swiftly toward Baltimore in an effort to reach New York or be picked up by the British fleet at some point on the Delaware. Some of the troops got over the river. However, as another wave of troops got under way, a severe storm arose which compelled them to return. The crossing had to be given up, and at dawn those who had reached Gloucester were brought back to man the crumbling works.

In the morning the batteries from the second parallel joined the others in raining death and destruction on the heads of the British. Continued resistance was useless. After the surrender, Cornwallis explained his plight to Clinton by writing: "We at this time could not fire a single gun, only one eight-inch and little more than an hundred cohorn shells remained . . ." Furthermore, his men were too exhausted to man the works any longer. "Under these circumstances, I thought it would have been wanton and inhuman to the last degree to sacrifice the lives of this small body of gallant soldiers . . ." (see Document 11).

Cornwallis Surrenders

At ten in the morning of October 17, a drummer boy appeared on the British rampart and beat a "parley." The cannonading stopped. The air, which a moment before was shaking like thunder, became as quiet as on a Sunday morning. Soon a British officer appeared with the drummer waving a white handkerchief. Washington immediately sent forward an officer who blindfolded the British officer and led him to the American lines. The blindfolds were removed, and the British officer handed Washington a note from Cornwallis. It read: "Sir, I propose a cessation of hostilities for twenty-four hours, and that two officers may be appointed by each side, to meet at Mr. Moore's house, to settle terms for the surrender of the forts at York and Gloucester."[6]

Washington answered: "An ardent desire to spare any further emission of blood, will readily incline me to listen to such terms."[7] However, he demanded that Cornwallis would send within two hours his proposals for surrender. The reply came within the appointed time. Cornwallis asked that his army upon surrender should be returned to England and Germany with the condition that none could serve again against America or France until exchanged.

Brushing aside Cornwallis's proposal, Washington the next day sent a letter stating his terms. The army would become prisoners of war but none would be returned to England or Germany. Furthermore, the same honors would be granted the garrison as had been received by the Americans at the surrender of Charleston in 1780. Cornwallis accepted the terms. He could do nothing else. The same day, commissioners consisting of Lt. Colonel Thomas Dundras and Major Alexander Ross for the British and Lt. Colonel John Laurens and the Viscount de Noailes for the Americans and French, met to frame the articles of surrender.

On the morning of October 19, the day of the surrender, Washington sent the articles of capitulation to Cornwallis for signing. In the articles were the stipulations for the formal surrender in the afternoon.

With all the pageantry of eighteenth-century war, the British marched out of Yorktown at two o'clock. The step of the weary and vanquished British was noticeably uneven as they marched with furled flags and the tune of bands appropriately playing "The World Turned Upside Down." On entering the surrender field, the British marched between the American and French troops drawn up for a mile on each side of the road. Not a word was uttered by the conquerors or the vanquished. Equally silent were the throngs of inhabitants who watched the unfolding spectacle in awe.

At the head of the British column rode General Charles O'Hara. But Cornwallis was not with his officers. He was sick, he said, and had deputized General O'Hara to surrender his sword. On reaching the cluster of American and French officers, O'Hara moved to present the sword to General Rochambeau, in an attempt to avoid the humiliation of surrendering to Washington. Count Mathieu Dumas, however, waved him on to Washington. The latter beckoned to General Lincoln to take the sword. Lincoln did so and then handed it back to O'Hara.

As the British soldiers filed past Washington and the officers, they were directed to a circle of Lauzun's Hussars to ground their arms. Many of the British and Hessians, wrote Dr. James Thatches, "manifested a sudden temper, throwing their arms on the pile with violence, as if determined to render them useless." This behavior, however, was soon stopped by an order from General Lincoln.

After the surrender, Washington and Rochambeau gave a reception and dinner for all higher officers, including those of the vanquished army. One could hardly imagine that only a few hours before, each side had been bent upon annihilating the other. Touched by the sympathy shown to his officers, Cornwallis wrote: "The treatment, in general, that we have received from the enemy since our surrender, has been perfectly good and proper, but the kindness and attention that has been shewn to us by the French officers in particular, their delicate sensibility of our situation, their generous and pressing offer of money both public and private, to any amount, has really gone beyond what I can possibly describe and will, I hope, make an impression on the breast of every British officer, whenever the fortune of war should put any of them into our power" (see Document 11).

It so happened that on the day of the surrender, Admiral Graves and General Clinton set sail with the fleet and six thousand troops to rescue Cornwallis.

Five days before, when Washington was bombarding Cornwallis into submission, Clinton wrote Cornwallis a letter containing several ways that his council of war had devised for rescuing Cornwallis. All called for the use of the fleet in the Chesapeake, but no word was said of how this could be accomplished. De Grasse had thirty-six ships of the line, eleven more than Graves's twenty-five. But Admiral Hood, ever ready to fight, believed the British fleet could force its way into the bay and rescue the fleet. Admiral Digby was very dubious.

It was about the time the drummer boy was beating the parley on the ramparts of the British works, that Graves's fleet filed out of New York Bay. It was not until the nineteenth that the fleet left Sandy Hook and headed south. Five days later, on reaching Cape Charles, a small boat was overtaken with three refugees from Yorktown who had escaped while the surrender was being negotiated. Their report of the surrender was soon confirmed. This time, Hood agreed with Graves that it was too risky to try to force an entrance into the Chesapeake and engage de Grasse. A few days later, the British fleet returned to New York. The Yorktown campaign had ended.

It was remarkable that during the entire campaign at Yorktown that virtually ended the war, the Americans and French consistently made what turned out to be the right moves at the right time. The British, however, on land and sea, made decisions which at the time appeared to be well-founded but in the end led to disaster. In the last analysis, the British failed because of vital miscalculations respecting naval strength in American waters.

Throughout history few great events have had the dramatic suspense which accompanied the Yorktown campaign. For weeks the alternatives of waging a New York campaign or one in Virginia, hung in the balance. Both had their advantages and disadvantages. Finally the riddle was solved, and Washington found the die cast in favor of Virginia. Success, however, still hinged upon Admiral de Grasse gaining and keeping control of the Chesapeake. When this was accomplished, Cornwallis's fate was sealed.

Notes

1. John C. Fitzpatrick, ed., *The Writing of George Washington*, 39 vols. (Washington, D.C.: Government Printing Office, 1931-1944), vol. 23, p. 119.

2. Ibid., p. 143.

3. John C. Fitzpatrick, ed., *George Washington's Diaries*, 4 vols. (Boston: Houghton Mifflin Co., 1925), vol. 2, p. 263.

4. B.F. Stevens, ed., *The Clinton-Cornwallis Controversy* (London, 1888), vol. 2, pp. 176-177.

5. John C. Fitzpatrick, *The Writings of George Washington*, vol. 23, pp. 227-228.

6. B.F. Stevens, ed., *The Clinton-Cornwallis Controversy*, vol. 2, p. 189.

7. Ibid., pp. 190-191.

Part two

Documents of the Decision

1

Washington's Situation in April, 1781: Letter to Laurens

Document†

[In cypher]
New Windsor, April 9, 1781.

The failure of this Expedition, (which was most flattering in the commencement of it) is much to be regretted; because a successful blow in that quarter, would, in all probability, have given a decisive turn to our Affairs in all the Southern States. Because it has been attended with considerable expence on our part, and much inconvenience to the State of Virginia, by assembling its Militia; and because the World are disappointed at not seeing Arnold in Gibbets. above all, because we stood in need of something to keep us a float, till the result of your mission is known for be assured my dear Laurens, that day does not follow night more certainly, than it brings with it some additional proof of the impracticability of carrying on the War without the aids you were directed to sollicit. As an honest and candid man; as a man whose all depends on the final and happy termination of the present contest, I assert this. While I give it decisively as my opinion, that without a foreign loan our present force (which is but the remnant of an Army) cannot be kept together this Campaign; much less will it be encreased, and in readiness for another. The observations contained in my letter to you of the 15th. of Jany. last, are verified every moment; And if France delays, a timely, and powerful aid in the critical posture of our affairs it will avail us nothing should she attempt it hereafter; for we are at this hour, suspended in the Balle; not from choice, but from hard and absolute necessity; for you may rely on it as a fact, that we cannot transport the provisions from the States in which they are Assessed to the Army, because we cannot pay the Teamsters, who will no longer work for Certificates. It is equally certain, that our Troops are approaching fast to nakedness and that we have nothing to cloath them with. That our Hospitals are without medicines, and our Sick without Nutriment, except such as well men eat. That all our public works are at a stand, and the

†From: John C. Fitzpatrick, ed., *The Writings of George Washington* (Washington, D.C.: Government Printing Office, 1931-1944), vol. xxi, pp. 438-39.

Artificers disbanding; but why need I run into the detail, when it may be declared in a word, that we are at the end of our tether, and that now or never our deliverance must come. While Alas! how easy would it be to retort the enemys own game upon them if it could be made to comport with the genl. plan of the War to keep a superior Fleet always in these Seas and France would put us in a conditn. to be active, by advancing us money. the ruin of the enemys schemes would then be certain; the bold game they are now playing would be the mean to effect it for they would be reduced to the necessity of concentering their force at capital points, thereby giving up all the advantages they have gained in the Southern States, or be vulnerable every where.

2

Cornwallis's Decision for Virginia: British Perceptions of the War

Document 2-a†

Clinton to Cornwallis, March, 1781

New York 2d & 5th March 1781.

My Lord,

I inclose your Lordship all the News I have been able to collect: Ethan Allen has I think quitted Congress and put them at Defiance. Your Lordship will see his Plan by the News Paper of the 28th February, said to to genuine. Discontent runs high in Connecticut. In short my Lord there seems nothing wanting to give a mortal Stab to Rebellion, but a proper Reinforcement and a permanent Superiority at Sea for the next Campaign, without which any Enterprize depending on Water Movements must certainly run great Risque. Shou'd the Troops already embarked for Chesapeak proceed, & When there, be able to undertake any Operation in addition to what Brigadier Genl. Arnold proposes; I am confident it will be done. Major Genl. Phillips will command this Expedition.

Document 2-b‡

Cornwallis to Germain, March, 1781

Guildford 17th March, 1781.

My Lord, I have the satisfaction to inform Your Lordship, that His Majesty's Troops under my command, obtained a signal Victory on the 15th Inst. over the Rebel Army, commanded by General Greene.

---

†From: B.F. Stevens, ed., *The Clinton-Cornwallis Controversy* (London, 1888), vol. 1, pp. 341-43.
‡From: Ibid., pp. 363-70.

In pursuance of my intended Plan, communicated to your Lordship in my Dispatch, No. 7, I had encamped on the 13th Inst at the Quaker Meeting, between the forks of Deep River. On the 14th I received information, that General Butler with a body of North-Carolina Militia, and the expected Reinforcements from Virginia, said to consist of a Virginia State Regiment, a Corps of Virginia eighteen months men, 3000 Virginia Militia, & Recruits for the Maryland Line, had joined General Greene; and that the whole Army, which was reported to amount to 9 or 10,000 men, was marching to attack the British Troops. During the Afternoon intelligence was brought, which was confirmed in the night, that he had advanced that day to Guildford, about 12 miles from our Camp. Being now persuaded that he had resolved to hazard an engagement; after detaching Lieut Colonel Hamilton with our Waggons, and Baggage, escorted by his own Regiment, a detachment of 100 Infantry, and 20 Cavalry, towards Bell's Mill on Deep River, I marched with the rest of the Corps, at day break, on the morning of the 15th, to meet the Enemy, or to attack them in their encampment. About four miles from Guildford, our advanced Guard, commanded by Lieut Colonel Tarleton, fell in with a Corps of the Enemy, consisting of Lee's Legion, some back Mountain Men, and Virginia Militia, which he attacked with his usual good conduct and spirit, and defeated: And continuing our March, we found the Rebel Army posted on rising Grounds about a mile and a half from the Court House. The Prisoners taken by Lieut Colonel Tarleton, having been several days with the advanced Corps, could give me no account of the Enemy's Order or position, and the Country people were extremely inaccurate in their description of the Ground. Immediately between the head of the Column, and the Enemy's Line, was a considerable Plantation, one large Field of which, was on our left of the Road, and two others, with a Wood of about two hundred yards broad between them, on our right of it; beyond these fields the Wood continued for several miles to our right. The Wood beyond the Plantation in our front, in the Skirt of which the Enemy's first Line was formed, was about a mile in depth, the road then leading into an extensive space of cleared Ground about Guildford Court House. The Woods on our right and left were reported to be impracticable for Cannon, but as that on our right, appeared to be most open, I resolved to attack the left Wing of the Enemy, and whilst my disposition was making for that purpose, I ordered Lieutenant Macleod to bring forward the Guns and cannonade their Center. The Attack was directed to be made in the following Order.

On the right, the Regiment of Bose, and the 71st Regiment, led by Major General Leslie, and supported by the 1st Battalion of Guards, on their left the 23rd and 33rd Regiments, led by Lieut Colonel Webster, & supported by the Grenadiers and 2nd Battalion of Guards, commanded by Brigadier General O'hara, The Yagers and Light Infantry of the Guards remained in the wood on the left of the Guns, and the Cavalry in the road, ready to act as circumstances might require. Our preparations being made, the Action began about half an hour past one in the afternoon; Major General Leslie after being obliged, by the great extent of the enemy's Line, to bring up the 1st Battalion of Guards to the right of the Regiment of Bose, soon defeated every thing before him; Lieut. Colonel Webster, having joined the left of Major General Leslie's division, was no less successfull in his front, when on finding that the left of the 33rd was exposed to a heavy fire from the right Wing of the Enemy, he changed his front to the Left, & being supported by the Yagers & Light Infantry of the Guards, attacked & routed it. The Grenadiers & 2nd Battalion of Guards, moving forward to occupy the Ground, left vacant by the movement of Lieut. Colonel Webster.

All the Infantry being now in the Line, Lieut. Colonel Tarleton, had directions to keep his Cavalry compact, and not to charge without positive orders, except to protect any of the Corps from the most evident danger of being defeated. The excessive thickness of the woods rendered our bayonets of little use, and enabled the broken enemy to make frequent stands, with an irregular fire, which occasioned some loss, and to several of the Corps, great delay, particularly on our right, when the 1st Battalion of Guards, and Regiment of Bose, were warmly engaged, in front, flank, & rear, with some of the enemy, that had been routed on the first attack, and with part of the extremity of their left wing, which by the closeness of the wood had been passed unbroken, The 71st Regiment, & Grenadiers & 2nd Battalion of Guards not knowing what was passing on their right, and hearing the fire advance on their left, continued to move forward, the Artillery keeping pace with them on the road followed by the Cavalry. The 2nd Battalion of Guards first gained the clear ground near Guildford Court house, and found a Corps of Continental Infantry, much superior in number, formed in the open field on the left of the Road. Glowing with impatience to signalize themselves, they instantly attacked and defeated them, taking two six pounders, but pursuing into the wood with too much ardour, were thrown into confusion by a heavy fire, and immediately charged and driven back into the field, by Colonel Washington's Dragoons, with the loss of the six pounders they had taken. The Enemy's Cavalry was soon repulsed, by a well directed fire from two three pounders, just brought up by Lieut. Macleod, & by the appearance of the Grenadiers of the Guards, and of the 71st Regiment which having been impeded by some deep Ravines, were now coming out of the wood, on the right of the Guards, opposite to the Court house. By the spirited exertions of Brigre. General O'hara, tho' wounded, the 2nd Battalion of Guards was soon rallied, & supported by the Grenadiers, returned to the charge with the greatest alacrity; The 23rd Regiment arriving at that instant from our left, & Lieut. Colonel Tarleton having advanced with part of the Cavalry, the enemy were soon put to flight, & the two six pounders once more fell into our hands, two Ammunition Waggons, & two other six pounders, being all the Artillery they had in the field, were likewise taken. About this time the 33rd Regiment and Light Infantry of the Guards, after overcoming many difficulties, completely routed the Corps, which was opposed to them, and put an end to the Action in this quarter; The 23rd & 71st Regiments, with part of the Cavalry, were ordered to pursue, the Remainder of the Cavalry was detached with Lieut.-Colonel Tarleton to our right, where a heavy fire still continued, and where his appearance & spirited attack, contributed much to a speedy termination of the action. The Militia with which our right had been engaged, dispersed in the woods, the Continentals went off by the Reedy Fork, beyond which, it was not in my power to follow them, as their Cavalry had suffered but little; our troops were excessively fatigued, by an action which lasted an hour & a half, and our numerous wounded, dispersed over an extensive space of Country, required immediate attention: The Care of our wounded, and the total want of provisions in an exhausted Country, made it equally impossible for me to follow the blow next day. The enemy did not stop untill they got to the Iron-works on Troublesome Creek, 18 miles from the field of Battle.

From our own observation, and the best accounts we could procure, we did not doubt but the Strength of the enemy exceeded 7,000 men; Their Militia composed their Line, with parties advanced to the Rails of the Fields in their front, the Continentals were posted obliquely in the rear of their right wing. Their Cannon fired on us, whilst we were forming, from the center of the Line of Militia but were withdrawn to the Continentals before the Attack.

I have the honour to inclose to your Lordship, the list of our killed and wounded; Captain Schutz's wound is supposed to be mortal, but the Surgeons assure me, that none of the other Officers are in danger, and that a great number of the men will soon recover. I cannot ascertain the loss of the enemy, but it must have been considerable, between 2 & 300 dead were left upon the field; many of their wounded that were able to move, whilst we were employed in the care of our own, escaped and followed the routed enemy; and our Cattle Drivers and foraging parties have reported to me, that the houses in a circle of 6 or 8 miles round us are full of others; Those that remained we have taken the best care of in our power. We took few prisoners, owing to the excessive thickness of the Wood facilitating their escape, and every man of our army being repeatedly wanted for Action.

The Conduct and Actions of the Officers and Soldiers, that compose this little Army will do more justice to their merit, than I can by words. Their persevering intrepidity in Action, their invincible patience in the hardships and fatigues of a march, of above 600 miles, in which they have forded several large Rivers, and numberless Creeks, many of which would be reckoned large rivers in any other Country in the world, without Tents or covering against the Climate, and often without provisions, will sufficiently manifest their ardent zeal for the honour and interests of their Sovereign and their Country.

I have been particularly indebted to Major General Leslie, for his gallantry and exertion in the Action, as well as his Assistance in every other part of the Service. The zeal & Spirit of Brigre. General O'hara, merit my highest commendations, for, after receiving two dangerous wounds, he continued in the field whilst the Action lasted; By his earnest attention on all other occasions, seconded by the Officers and Soldiers of the Brigade, His Majesty's Guards are no less distinguished by their order and discipline, than by their Spirit and valour.

The Hessian Regiment of Bose deserves my warmest praises for it's discipline alacrity and Courage, and does honour to Major Du Buy who commands it, and who is an Officer of superior merit.

I am much obliged to Brigadier General Howard, who served as Volunteer, for his spirited example on all occasions.

Lieut. Colonel Webster conducted his Brigade like an Officer of experience and Gallantry. Lieut. Colonel Tarleton's good conduct & spirit in the management of his Cavalry, was conspicuous during the whole action; & Lieut. Macleod, who commanded the Artillery, proved himself, upon this, as well as all former occasions, a most capable & deserving Officer. The attention and exertion of my Aids-de-Camp, and of all the other publick Officers of the Army, contributed very much to the success of the day.

I have constantly received the most zealous assistance from Governor Martin, during my command in the southern district, hoping that his presence would tend to incite the loyal Subjects of this Province to take an active part with us, he has chearfully submitted to the fatigues and dangers of our Campaign, but his delicate constitution has suffered by his publick spirit, for by the advice of the Physicians, he is now obliged to return to England for the recovering his health.

This part of the Country is so totally destitute of subsistence, that forage is not nearer than nine miles, and the Soldiers have been two days without bread; I shall therefore leave about 70 of the worst of the wounded cases, at the New Garden Quaker Meeting house, with proper Assistance, & move the remainder with the Army to-morrow morning to Bell's Mill. I hope our friends will heartily take an active part with us, to which I shall continue to encourage them; still approaching our shipping by easy marches, that we may procure the necessary Supplies for further operations, and lodge our sick and wounded, where proper attention can be paid to them.

This Dispatch will be delivered to Your Lordship by my Aide-de-Camp Captain Brodrick, who is a very promising Officer, and whom I beg leave to recommend to Your Lordship's Countenance and Favour.

I have the honour to be with great respect My Lord Your Lordship's Most obedient & Most humble Servant

CORNWALLIS.

Document 2-c†

Cornwallis to Germain, April, 1781

Wilmington 23 April 1781.

My Lord, I yesterday received an express, by a small Vessel from Charlestown, informing me, that a Frigate was there, but not then able to get over the bar, with Dispatches from Sir Henry Clinton, Notifying to me, that Major General Phillips, had been detached into the Chesapeak, with a

†From: Ibid., pp. 420-22.

considerable force, with instructions to co-operate with this Army, & to put himself under my orders. This Express likewise brought me the disagreeable accounts, that the upper posts of South Carolina, were in the most imminent danger from an alarming Spirit of Revolt among many of the people, and by a movement of Genl. Greene's Army.

Although the expresses I sent from Cross Creek, to inform Lord Rawdon of the necessity I was under of coming to this place, and to warn him of the possibility of such an attempt of the Enemy, had all miscarried, Yet his Lordship was lucky enough to be apprized of General Greene's Approach, at least six days before he could possibly reach Camden, and I am therefore still induced to hope from my opinion of His Lordship's Abilities, & the precautions taken by him, & Lieut. Colonel Balfour, that we shall not be so unfortunate, as to lose any considerable Corps.

The distance from hence to Camden, the want of forage and subsistence, on the greatest part of the Road, and the difficulty of passing the Pedee, when opposed by an Enemy, render it utterly impossible for me to give immediate assistance, And I apprehend a possibility of the utmost hazard to this little Corps, without the chance of a benefit, in the attempt; For if we are so unlucky, as to suffer a severe blow in South Carolina, the spirit of Revolt in that Province, would become very general, and the numerous Rebels in this Province, be encouraged to be more than ever active & violent; This might enable General Greene to hem me in among the great Rivers, & by cutting off our subsistence, render our Arms useless. And to remain here for Transports to carry us off, would be a work of time, would lose our Cavalry, & be otherways as ruinous and disgracefull to Britain, as most events could be. I have therefore, under so many embarrassing circumstances, (but looking upon Charlestown as safe from any immediate Attack from the Rebels) resolved to take advantage of General Greene's having left the back part of Virginia open, and march immediately into that province, to attempt a junction with General Phillips.

I have more readily decided upon this measure because if General Greene fails in the object of his March, his retreat will relieve South Carolina; And my force being very insufficient for offensive operations in this province may be employed usefully in Virginia, in conjunction with the Corps under the Command of General Phillips.

I have the honour to be with great respect My Lord Your Lordship's Most obedient and Most humble Servant

                                        CORNWALLIS.

Document 2-d†

Cornwallis to Clinton, May, 1781

                                Byrd's Plantation, North of
                                James River. 26 May 1781.

Sir. The Reinforcement is safely arrived in James River, and I opened all your dispatches to poor Phillips, marked *On His Majesty's Service.*

†From: Ibid., vol. 2, pp. 487-91.

I hope that your Excellency has received my Letters from Wilmington, and one of the 20th from Petersburgh; as the latter went by an uncertain conveyance, I send a duplicate of it.

The arrival of the reinforcement, has made me easy about Portsmouth, for the present, I have sent General Leslie thither with the 17th Regt. and the two Battalions of Anspach, keeping the 43rd Regiment with the Army.

I shall now proceed to dislodge La Fayette from Richmond, and with my light Troops to destroy any Magazines or Stores in the Neighbourhood, which may have been collected, either for his use or for General Greene's Army, From thence I purpose to move to the Neck at Williamsburgh, which is represented as healthy, & where some subsistence may be procured, and keep myself unengaged from operations, which might interfere with your plan for the Campaign, untill I have the Satisfaction of hearing from you. I hope I shall then have an opportunity to receive better information, than has hitherto been in my power to procure, relative to a proper harbour, & place of Arms: At present I am inclined to think well of York: The objections to Portsmouth are, that it cannot be made strong, without an Army to defend it, that it is remarkably unhealthy, and can give no protection to a Ship of the Line. Wayne has not yet joined La Fayette, nor can I positively learn where he is, nor what is his force. Greene's Cavalry are said to be coming this way, but I have no certain accounts of it.

Your Excellency desires Generals Phillips & Arnold to give you their opinion relative to Mr. *Alexander's* proposal; As General Arnold goes to New York by the first safe conveyance, you will have an opportunity of hearing his sentiments in person; Experience has made me less sanguine, and more Arrangements seem to me necessary, for so important an expedition, than appear to occur to General Arnold.

Mr. Alexander's conversations bear too strong a resemblance to those of the emissaries from North Carolina, to give me much confidence, and from the experience I have had, and dangers I have undergone, one maxim appears to me to be absolutely necessary for the safe & honourable conduct of this War, which is, that we should have as few posts as possible, & that wherever the King's Troops are, they should be in respectable force; By the vigorous exertions of the present Governors of America, large Bodies of men are soon collected, and I have too often observed, that when a Storm threatens, our friends disappear.

In regard to taking possession of Philadelphia by an incursion, (even if practicable) without an intention of keeping or burning it, (neither of which appear to be adviseable) I should apprehend, it would do more harm than good to the cause of Britain.

I shall take the liberty of repeating, that if offensive War is intended, Virginia appears to me, to be the only Province, in which it can be carried on, and in which there is a Stake; But to reduce the Province & keep possession of the Country, a considerable Army would be necessary, for with a small force, the business would probably terminate unfavourably, tho' the beginning might be successfull. In case it is thought expedient, & a proper Army for the attempt can be formed, I hope your Excellency will do me the justice to believe, that I neither wish nor expect to have the command of it, leaving you at New York on the defensive, such sentiments are so far from my heart, that I can with great truth assure you, that few things could give me greater pleasure, than being relieved by your presence, from a situation of so much anxiety & responsibility.

By my Letter of the 20th, your Excellency will observe, that instead of thinking it possible to do anything in North Carolina, I am of opinion that it is doubtfull, whether we can keep the posts in the back part of South Carolina, and I believe I have stated in former letters, the infinite difficulty of protecting a frontier of three hundred miles, against a persevering Enemy, in a country where we have no water communication, and where few of the Inhabitants are active or usefull friends.

In enumerating the Corps employ'd in the southern district, Your Excellency will recollect that they are all very weak, and that some of the British as well as provincial Regiments, retain nothing but the Name. Our weakness at Guildford was not owing to any detachment, unless that with the Baggage, but to our losses by action, Sickness &c during the Winter's Campaign.

I saw with concern, that You thought Lieut. Colonel Balfour had acted injudiciously, in sending home some Transports; that business has, I apprehend, been misrepresented by persons, interested in retaining rotten Vessels in the Service of Government; The circumstances I do not now perfectly recollect, but I believe you will find, that the Ships sent home, were either Victuallers, which the Treasury desired in the strongest manner, or Transports, which were so exceedingly bad, that they could never have gone out with safety, after a stay of three months in Charlestown harbour; Whatever was done in it, was with my approbation at the time, appearing evidently for the good of the Service, I therefore think it my duty to exculpate Lieut. Colonel Balfour, whom I have found on all occasions, a most zealous, intelligent, and deserving Officer.

Colonel Robinson's Corps is so weak & deserts so fast, that at the recommendation of General Arnold, I have consented that it shall return in the Transports to New York.

I have the honour to be with great respect Sir Your most obedient & most humble Servant

CORNWALLIS.

Document 2-e†

Clinton to Cornwallis, May, 1781

New-York, May 29th, 1781.

My Lord, I had the honour of writing to your Lordship by Lord Chewton, who sailed from hence in the Richmond the 4th instant, to join you at

†From: Ibid., vol. 1, pp. 493-98.

Wilmington; but your Lordship's departure from thence will have prevented his meeting you there, and I hope he has since then joined you in the Chesapeak.

When I first heard of your Lordship's retreat from Cross Creek to Wilmington, I confess that I was in hopes you had reason to consider Greene so totally *hors de combat* as to be perfectly at ease for Lord Rawdon's safety. And after your arrival at Wilmington I flattered myself that, if any change of circumstances should make it necessary, you could always have been able to march to the Walkamaw, where I imagined vessels might have passed you over to George-town. I cannot therefore conceal from your Lordship the apprehensions I felt on reading your letter to me of the 24th ult. wherein you inform me of the critical situation which you supposed the Carolinas to be in, and that you should probably attempt to effect a junction with Major-general Phillips.

Lord Rawdon's officer-like and spirited exertions, in taking advantage of Greene's having detached from his army, have indeed eased me of my apprehensions for the present. But in the disordered state of Carolina and Georgia, as represented to me by Lieutenant-colonel Balfour, I shall dread what may be the consequence of your Lordship's move, unless a reinforcement arrives very soon in South Carolina, and such instructions are sent to the officer commanding there, as may induce him to exert himself in restoring tranquillity in that province at least. These I make no doubt your Lordship has already sent to Lord Rawdon, and that every necessary measure for this purpose will be taken by his Lordship in consequence of them, should he remain in the command. But as there are many officers in the regiments coming out who are older than Lord Rawdon, I have to lament the probability of his being superseded in it, as I can scarce flatter myself that any of them will be possessed of the knowledge requisite for conducting operations in Carolina without having ever served in that country, or be so competent to the command there as officers of more local experience. I therefore beg leave to submit to your Lordship the propriety of sending either Major-general Leslie or Brigadier-general O'Hara to Charles-town, to take the command of the troops in that district; which in the present critical situation of affairs in the Southern Colonies, will certainly require an officer of experience, and a perfect knowledge of the country. Had it been possible for your Lordship in your letter to me of the 10th ult. to have intimated the probability of your intention to form a junction with General Phillips, I should certainly have endeavoured to have stopped you, as I did then, as well as now, consider such a move as likely to be dangerous to our interests in the Southern Colonies. And this, my Lord, was not my only fear; for I will be free to own, that I was apprehensive for the corps under your Lordships immediate orders, as well as for that under Lord Rawdon: and I should not have thought even the one under Major-general Phillips in safety at Petersburg, at least for so long a time, had I not fortunately on hearing of your being at Wilmington sent another detachment from this army to reinforce him.

I am persuaded your Lordship will have the goodness to excuse my saying thus much; but what is done, cannot now be altered: and as your Lordship has thought proper to make this decision, I shall most gladly avail myself of your very able assistance in carrying on such operations as you shall judge best in Virginia, until we are compelled, as I fear we must be, by the climate, to bring them more northward. Your Lordship will have been informed of my ideas respecting operations to the northward of the Carolinas, by my instructions to the different General officers detached to the Chesapeak; and the substance of some conversations with General Phillips on that subject, which I committed to writing and sent to him with my last dispatch, with directions to communicate it to your Lordship. By these your Lordship will observe that my first object has ever been a co-operation with your measures; but your Lordship's situation at different periods, made it necessary for me occasionally to vary my instructions to those General officers according to circumstances. They were originally directed to assist your Lordship's operations in securing South and recovering North Carolina; their attention was afterwards pointed to the saving South Carolina; and now your Lordship may possibly think it necessary to employ your force in recovering both or either of those provinces, by either a direct or indirect operation. With respect to the first, your Lordship must be the sole judge; with respect to the last, you have my opinions, which may however probably give way to yours, should they differ from them, as they will have the advantage of being formed on the spot, and upon circumstances, which at this distance I cannot of course judge of: I shall therefore leave them totally to your Lordship to decide upon, until you either hear from me or we meet.

I should be happy to be able to ascertain the time when our reinforcements may arrive; but as I have received no letters from the minister of a later date than the 7th of February, I am at a loss to guess how soon we may expect them. As I had judged the force I sent to the Chesapeak fully sufficient for all operations there, even though we should extend them to the Experiment (mentioned in the conversations referred to) at the Western Head of Chesapeak about Baltimore, &c. and your Lordship will perceive that it was Generals Phillips and Arnold's opinion, they were sufficient for even that on the Eastern; (which however might certainly require a much greater force,) it is possible that the additional corps your Lordship has brought with you, may enable you to return something to me for this post: but I beg your Lordship will by no means consider this as a call; for I would rather content myself with ever so bare a defensive, until there was an appearance of serious operations against me, than cramp yours in the least. But (as I said in a former letter) I trust to your Lordship's disinterestedness, that you will not require from me more troops than are absolutely wanted; and that you will recollect a circumstance, which I am ever aware of in carrying on operations in the Chesapeak, which is, that they can be no longer secure than whilst we are superior at sea. That we shall remain so, I most sincerely hope; nor have I any reason to suspect we shall not: but at all events, I may at least expect timely information will be sent me of the contrary being likely to happen. In which case I hope your Lordship may be able to place your army in a secure situation during such temporary inconvenience; for should it become permanent I need not say what our prospects in this country are likely to be. The Admiral being now off the Hook, gives me an opportunity of communicating with him by letter; and I have in the most pressing terms requested his attention to the Chesapeak, having repeatedly told him, that should the enemy possess it even for forty-eight hours your Lordship's operations there may be exposed to most imminent danger. General Robertson has also endeavoured to impress him with the same ideas; but until I have an answer in writing I cannot be sure that he will, as I do, consider the Chesapeak as the first object. For he at present seems rather inclined to lead his fleet to open the Port of Rhode-Island, and to cruise to the northward of Nantucket, for a fleet which he has heard is coming from Europe with a small reinforcement to the French armament, and which I am of opinion is bound to Rhode-Island. I have, however, taken every occasion to represent to him the necessity of hearty co-operation and communication; if they fail, I am determined it shall not be on my side.

The requisitions your Lordship has made in your letter to me of the 20th instant, for horse accoutrements, &c. shall be supplied to the utmost extent of our abilities; and the inclosed extracts of letters from Leitenant-colonel Innes to his deputy at Charlestown, &c. will explain to your Lordship why they are not more ample.

June 1st. I have this moment received the Admiral's answer to my letter; and I am to suppose from it that he will do everything in his power to guard the Chesapeak. The copy is inclosed for your Lordship's information. I heartily wish he may continue in this disposition; the necessity of which I shall not fail to urge by every opportunity he may give me of communicating with him.

As I shall frequently send one of my advice boats to your Lordship with any information which may deserve your attention, I hope to hear from you by the same conveyance. Lord Chewton has a cypher, which was given him for that purpose; but should he not have joined you, we may make use of Colonel Dundas's until he does.

I shall spare your Lordship and myself the pain of saying much to you on the loss of our valuable friend; I feel it too sensibly for expression.

I have the honour to be, &c.

H. CLINTON.

Document 2-f†

Clinton to Cornwallis, June, 1781

New-York, June 15, 1781.

[Received June 26, 1781, from Ensign Amiel.]

My Lord, As the Admiral has thought proper to stop the sailing of the convoy with stores, horse accoutrements, &c. (which has been for some days

†From: Ibid., vol. 2, pp. 24-25

ready to sail to the Chesapeak) without assigning to me any reason for so doing, I delay not a moment to dispatch a runner to your Lordship, with a duplicate of my letter of the 11th instant, which was to go by that opportunity.

And as I am led to suppose (from your Lordship's letter of the 26th ult.) that you may not think it expedient to adopt the operations I had recommended in the Upper Chesapeak, and will be this time probably have finished those you were engaged in, I request you will immediately embark a part of the troops stated in the letter inclosed (beginning with the light infantry, &c.) and send them to me with all possible dispatch; for which purpose, Captain Hudson, or officer commanding the King's ships, will I presume, upon your Lordship's application appoint a proper convoy.

I shall likewise in proper time solicit the Admiral to send some more transports to the Chesapeak, in which your Lordship will please to send hither the remaining troops you judge can be spared from the defence of the posts you may occupy; as I do not think it advisable to leave more troops in that unhealthy climate at this season of the year than what are absolutely wanted for a defensive, and desultory water excursions.

I have the honour to be, &c.

H. CLINTON.

Document 2-g†

Clinton to Cornwallis, June, 1781
New York, 19th of June, 1781.

My Lord, The intercepted letters, which I had the honour to transmit to your Lordship with my dispatch of the 8th inst. will have informed you, that the French Admiral meant to escape with his fleet to Boston, from Rhode Island; (from whence it is probable they sailed the 15th inst. the wind being then fair;) and that it was proposed the French army should afterwards join such troops as Mr. Washington could assemble, for the purpose of making an attempt on this post.

I have often given it as my opinion to your Lordship, that for such an object as this, they certainly could raise numbers; but I very much doubt their being able to feed them. I am, however, persuaded, they will attempt the investiture of the place. I therefore heartily wish I was more in force, that I might be able to take advantage of any false movement they may make in forming it.

Should your Lordship have any solid operation in the Chesapeak to propose, or have approved of the one I mentioned in my former letters, I shall not, as I have already told you, press you for the corps I wished to have sent me, at least for the present. But if, in the approaching inclement season, your Lordship should not think it prudent to undertake operations with the troops you have, (and you may easily conceive I cannot possibly spare more,)

†From: Ibid., pp. 26-28.

I cannot but wish for their sake, if I had no other motive, that you would send me as soon as possible what you can spare from a respectable defensive. And that your Lordship may better judge what I mean by a *respectable* defensive, it is necessary to inform you, that other intelligence, besides Monsieur Barras' letter, makes it highly probable, that Monsieur de Grasse, will visit this coast in the hurricane season, and bring with him troops as well as ships. But, when he hears that your Lordship has taken possession of York river before him, I think it most likely he will come to Rhode Island; and, in that case, that their first efforts will be in this quarter. I am, however, under no great apprehensions, as Sir George Rodney seems to have the same suspicions of De Grasse's intention that we have, and will of course follow him hither. For I think our situation cannot become very critical, unless the enemy by having the command of the Sound, should possess themselves of Long Island; which can never be the case, whilst we are superior at sea.

What I said to your Lordship in my letter of the 8th inst. respecting the reinforcement from England, was only occasioned by a report prevailing here, that you had ordered them from Charles-town to the Chesapeak. But as it is now probable there is no real foundation for the report, it is unnecessary to trouble your Lordship again on the subject, as they will of course remain in South Carolina, should they arrive there. In the hope that your Lordship will be able to spare me three thousand men, I have sent two thousand tons of transports from hence; and what is wanting may be made up from those in Chesapeak. The corps I named in my letter of the 11th, will, I imagine, amount to nearly that number. But should your Lordship not be able to spare the whole, it is necessary to mention, that I expect the detachment of the seventeenth dragoons, as they happened to be placed last in the list. I likewise request, your Lordship will at the same time send me the twenty-four boats built by General Arnold, if you should have no particular call for them; as they will be useful here, and it is probable the ten, (which I understand are now building in the Chesapeak, will be sufficient for your Lordship's purposes. But as your Lordship will be the best judge of this, you will send them or not, as you please.

I have at least had a personal conference with the Vice-admiral; and he has agreed, if he does not intercept the French fleet, to take his station between the Nantucket Shoals and Delaware, where his fleet is to cruise for the protection of this harbour, and our communication with the Chesapeak.

I have the honour to be, &c.

H. CLINTON.

Document 2-h†

Clinton to Cornwallis, June, 1781.

New-York, June 28, 1781. [In Cypher.]
My Lord, Having for very essential reasons come to a resolution of endeavouring by a rapid move to seize the stores, &c. collected at

†From: Ibid., pp. 29-30.

Philadelphia, and afterwards to bring the troops employed on that service to reinforce this post, I am to request, that if your Lordship has not already embarked the reinforcement I called for in my letters of the 8th, 11th, 15th, and 19th instant, and should not be engaged in some very important move, either of your own, or in consequence of my ideas respecting operation in the Upper-Chesapeak, you will be pleased, as soon as possible, to order an embarkation of the troops ... and of stores, &c. &c. stated in the enclosed paper; — or, in as full a manner as your Lordship can with propriety comply; — recollecting, that whatever may have been taken too great a proportion of, will be immediately returned to you the moment the expedition is over.

As it is possible that your Lordship may have sent Major-general Leslie to Charles-town, in consequence of what I said to you in my letter of the 29th ult. I have thought proper to appoint General Robertson to the command of the troops on this service, which I should not have judged necessary, could I have been certain of his being named by you to accompany the troops coming hither. Should that have been the case, your Lordship will be pleased, nevertheless, to direct him to proceed with the expedition.

I have the honour to be, &c.

H. CLINTON.

3

The British Fortify Yorktown: Disagreements Between Cornwallis and Clinton

Document 3-a†

Cornwallis to Clinton, June 30, 1781

Earl Cornwallis to Sir Henry Clinton
Williamsburgh 30th June 1781.

Sir, After passing James river at Westover, I moved to Hanover Court-house, and crossed the South Anna; the Marquis de La fayette marched to his Left, keeping above me at the distance of about twenty miles.

By pushing my light Troops over the North Anna, I alarmed the Enemy for Fredericksburgh, & for the junction with General Wayne, who was then marching through Maryland. From what I could learn of the present state of Hunter's Iron Manufactory, it did not appear of so much importance as the stores on the other side of the Country, and it was impossible to prevent the junction between the Marquis & Wayne; I therefore took the advantage of the Marquis's passing the Rappahanock, and detached Lieut.-Colonels Simcoe & Tarleton to disturb the Assembly, then sitting at Charlotteville, and to destroy the Stores there, at Old Albermarle Court-House, & the Point of Fork, moving with the Infantry to the mouth of Bird Creek, near the Point of Fork, to receive those detachments. Lieut. Colonel Tarleton took some Members of the Assembly at Charlotteville, & destroyed there, & on his return, 1000 stand of good Arms, some Clothing & other stores, & between 4 or 500 barrels of powder, without opposition. Baron Steuben, who commanded about 800 twelvemonth's-men & Militia, retired with great precipitation from the Point of Fork. Lieut. Colonel Simcoe after using every exertion to attack his rear-Guard, destroyed there, & at places adjacent, about 3300 stand of Arms, most of which unserviceable, but then under repair, some Salt, Harness, &c. & about 150 Barrels of Powder. I then moved by

†From: Ibid., pp. 31-38.

Richmond, & arrived at Williamsburgh on the 25th Inst., having in addition to the Articles already mentioned, destroyed on this expedition, at different places above 2000 Hogsheads of Tobacco, & a great number of Iron Guns, & brought off 4 brass 13 inch Mortars, 5 brass 8 inch Howitzers, & four long brass nine-pounders, all french. We found near Hanover Court-house, ten french brass 24 pounders, which we could not carry, & had not time or means to destroy further than spiking, & throwing five or six of them into the Pamunkey; and we found at Williamsburgh a considerable quantity of Shot & Shells, which are embarked. General Wayne joined the Marquis about the middle of the Month, as did Baron Steuben soon after, and their Army has generally kept about twenty Miles from us, without any material attempt by detachment, except in an attack on Lieut. Colonel Simcoe, on the 26th, as he was returning with his Corps & the Yagers, from the destruction of some boats & Stores on the Chickahominy; The Enemy tho' much superior in numbers, were repulsed with considerable Loss, 3 officers & 28 private were made prisoners: The Rangers had 3 officers & 30 private killed & wounded. Lieut. Jones, who was killed, behaved with great spirit, & is much lamented by Lieut. Colonel Simcoe.

The Morning after my arrival here, I was honoured with your Excellency's Dispatches of the 11th & 15th inst., delivered by Ensign Amiel; By them I find, that you think if an offensive Army could be spared, it would not be adviseable to employ it in this Province. It is natural for every Officer to turn his thoughts particularly to the part of the War, in which he has been most employed; and as the security at least of South Carolina, if not the reduction of North Carolina, seemed to be generally expected from me, both in this Country & in England, I thought myself called upon, after the experiment I had made, had failed, to point out the only mode in my opinion of effecting it; and to declare, that untill Virginia was to a degree subjected, we could not reduce North Carolina, or have any certain hold of the back Country of South Carolina; The want of Navigation rendering it impossible to maintain a sufficient Army in either of these Provinces at a considerable distance from the Coast, & the Men & Riches of Virginia furnishing ample supplies to the Rebel Southern Army. I will not say much in praise of the Militia of the Southern Colonies, but the List of British Officers & Soldiers killed & wounded by them, since last June, proves but too fatally that they are not wholly contemptible.

Your Excellency being charged with the Weight of the whole American War, your opinions of course are less partial and are directed to all its parts; to those opinions it is my duty implicitly to submit.

Being in the place of General Phillips, I thought myself called upon by you, to give my opinion with all deference, on Mr. Alexander's proposals, & the Attempt upon Philadelphia. Having experienced much disappointment on that head, I own, I would cautiously engage in measures, depending materially for their success upon active assistance from the Country; and I thought the Attempt upon Philadelphia, would do more harm than good to the cause of Britain, Because, supposing it practicable to get possession of the Town, (which, besides other obstacles, if the Redoubts are kept up, would not be easy) we could not hope to arrive, without their having had sufficient Warning of our approach, to enable them to secure Specie, & the greatest part of their valuable publick Stores, by means of their Boats & Shipping, which give them certain possession of the River from Mud Island upwards; The discriminating of the Owners, & destroying any considerable quantity of West India Goods, & other Merchandize, dispersed thro' a great Town, without burning the whole together, would be a work of much time & labour; Our appearance there, without an intention to stay, might give false hopes to many friends, & occasion their ruin; and any unlucky accident on our Retreat, might furnish matter for great triumph to our enemies; However, my opinion on that subject is, at present, of no great importance, as it appears, from your Excellency's Dispatches, that, in the execution of those Ideas, a Co-operation was intended from your side, which now could not be depended upon, from the uncertainty of the permanency of our Naval Superiority, and your apprehensions of an intended serious attempt upon New York: I have, therefore, lost no time in taking measures for complying with the Requisition contained in your dispatch of the 15th instant.

Upon viewing York, I was clearly of opinion, that it far exceeds our power, consistent with your plans to make safe defensive posts there & at Gloucester, both of which would be necessary for the protection of Shipping. The State of the Transports has not yet been reported to me, but I have ordered the few that are at Portsmouth, to be got ready, and as soon as I pass James River, (for which purpose the Boats are collecting) & can get a Convoy, they shall be dispatched with as many troops, as they will contain, & shall be followed by others, as fast as you send Transports to receive them. When I see Portsmouth, I shall give my opinion of the Number of Men necessary for it's defence, or of any other post that may be thought more proper. But as Magazines, &c. may be destroyed by occasional expeditions from New York, and there is little chance of being able to establish a post capable of giving effectual protection to Ships of War, I submit it to your Excellency's consideration, whether it is worth while to hold a sickly defensive post in this Bay, which will always be exposed to a sudden French Attack, and, which experience has now shewn, makes no diversion in favour of the Southern Army.

Tarleton was lucky enough to intercept an Express with Letters from Greene & La fayette, of which the inclosed are Copies. By them you will see General Greene's intention of coming to the Northward, & that part of the Reinforcements, destined for his Army, was stopped in consequence of my Arrival here, there can be little doubt of his returning to the Southward, & of the Reinforcements proceeding to join his Army.

I still continue in the most painfull Anxiety for the situation of South Carolina; Your Excellency will have received accounts of Lord

Rawdon's proceedings, previous to his Arrival at Monk's Corner, & of his intended operations. My last account from him, is in a Note to Lieut. Colonel Balfour, dated the 9th Inst. at Four hole Bridge, and he was then in great hopes of being in time to save Cruger. I have ordered Colonel Gould to proceed as soon as Convoy could be procured with the 19th & 30th Regiments to New York, leaving the 3rd Regiment & Flank Companies in South Carolina, till your pleasure be known. I named the Flank Companies, because they might be distant at the time of the arrival of the order, & as a Corps capable of exertion is much wanted on that Service.

Your Excellency well knows my opinion of a defensive War on the Frontiers of South Carolina. From the state of Lord Rawdon's health, it is impossible that he can remain, for which reason, altho' the Command in that quarter can only be attended with Mortification & disappointment; yet, as I came to America with no other view, than to endeavour to be usefull to my Country, and as I do not think it possible to render any Service in a defensive situation here, I am willing to repair to Charlestown if you approve of it, & in the mean time, I shall do every thing in my power to arrange Matters here, till I have your answer.

Major Craig represented so strongly to Lord Rawdon his regret at leaving the distressed Loyalists in the Neighbourhood of Wilmington, & his hopes of a considerable insurrection in the lower part of North Carolina, where the Enemy have no force, that His Lordship gave him a conditional permission, to postpone the evacuation of Wilmington; but I have not yet learned, whether he has availed himself of it.

La fayette's Continentals, I believe, consist of about 17 or 1800 men, exclusive of some twelvemonth's men, collected by Steuben; He has received considerable Reinforcements of Militia, & about 800 Mountain Rifle-Men under Campbell; He keeps with his Main Body about 18 or 20 miles from us, his advanced Corps about 10 or 12, probably with an intention of insulting our Rear Guard, when we pass James River; I hope, however, to put that out of his power, by crossing at James City Island; and if I can get a favourable opportunity of striking a blow at him without loss of time, I will certainly try it. I will likewise attempt Water expeditions, if proper objects present themselves, after my arrival at Portsmouth.

I inclose a Report made by Lieut. Thomas Hagerty, who came with a Captain Fleming from Maryland to join us in North Carolina. I feel most sincerely for the Sufferings of the unfortunate Loyalists; but being of opinion, that a detachment would not afford them substantial & permanent relief, I shall not venture such a step, unless your Excellency should think proper to direct it.

I have the honour to be, with great respect, Sir Your most obedient & Most humble Servant

CORNWALLIS.

Document 3-b†

Clinton to Cornwallis, July, 1781

Head-Quarters, New-York, July 8th, 1781.

[Received July 21st, 1781, from Captain Stapleton.]

My Lord, I am this moment honoured with your Lordship's letter by Ensign Amiel of the 30th ultimo, and am very happy to be informed you have had an opportunity of destroying such a quantity of arms and public stores, the loss of which must be very heavily felt by the enemy.

By your Lordship's answer to my letters of the 11th and 15th ultimo, (which are the only ones you acknowledge the receipt of, and in which I made a requisition for some of the corps serving in the Chesapeak, *if you could spare them,*) I am to understand that your Lordship does not think, that with the remainder (which would have amounted to at least four thousand, supposing even that you sent me three thousand,) you could maintain the posts I had proposed to be occupied at York-town, &c. so necessary in every respect to cover our fleet, and give us entire command over the entrance of that bay. I therefore think proper to mention to your Lordship, that whatever my ideas may have been of the force sufficient to maintain that station, and the corresponding one on the Gloucester side, your Lordship was left the sole judge of that sufficiency to the whole amount of the corps under your immediate orders in Virginia; nor did I mean to draw a single man from you until you had provided for a respectable defensive, and retained a small corps for desultory water expeditions; for my requisition was made after the receipt of your Lordship's letter of the 26th of May; from which I apprehend that you had no immediate operation of your own to propose, and did not think it expedient to adopt the one I had recommended to General Phillips. But I confess I could not conceive you would require above four thousand in a station wherein General Arnold had represented to me (upon report of Colonel Simcoe) that two thousand men would be amply sufficient; and being strongly impressed with the necessity of our holding a naval station for large ships as well as small, and judging that York-town was of importance for securing such a one, I cannot but be concerned that your Lordship should so suddenly lose sight of it, pass James-river, and retire with your army to the sickly post of Portsmouth, where your horses will, I fear, be starved, and a hundred other inconveniences will attend you: and this, my Lord, as you are pleased to say, because you were of opinion that it exceeded your power, consistent with my plans, to make safe defensive posts there and at Gloucester. My plans, my Lord, were to draw from Chesapeak, as well for the sake of their health, as for a necessary defensive in this important post, such troops as your Lordship could spare from a respectable defensive of York, Gloucester, or such other station as was proper to cover line of battle ships, and all the other services I had recommended; but I could not possibly mean that your Lordship should, for this, give up the hold of a station so

†From: Ibid., pp. 49-50.

important for the purposes I designed, and which I think La Fayette will immediately seize and fortify the moment he hears you have repassed James-river; for though I am to suppose the enemy will be as little able to defend it with five thousand as your Lordship judges yourself to be, and of course may be for the same reasons dispossessed, I should be sorry to begin with a siege the operations I am determined to carry on in Chesapeak whenever the season will admit of it; I will therefore consult Rear-admiral Graves on this subject, and let your Lordship have our joint opinion in consequence.

With regard to Portsmouth, your Lordship will have seen by my former letters and the papers in your possession, that when I sent General Leslie to the Chesapeak, I only wished for a station to cover our cruising frigates and other small ships; that General officer thought proper to make choice of Portsmouth, and had, I doubt not, good reasons for so doing. But it has ever been my opinion that if a better could be found, especially for covering line of battle ships, it ought to have the preference; and I think, if Old Point Comfort will secure Hampton-Road, that is the station we ought to choose; for if Elizabeth-River is at all kept, a small post for about three hundred men at Mill-Point, would in my opinion answer. But as to quitting the Chesapeak entirely, I cannot entertain a thought of such a measure, but shall most probably on the contrary send there, as soon as the season returns for acting in that climate, all the troops which can possibly be spared from the different posts under my command. I therefore flatter myself, that even although your Lordship may have quitted York and detached troops to me, that you will have a sufficiency to re-occupy it, or that you will at least hold Old Point Comfort, if it is possible to do it without York.

I find by the intercepted letters you sent me, that La Fayette's continentals, when joined by Stuben and Wayne, do not altogether exceed one thousand eight hundred, and that if he could collect a numerous militia, he had but few arms to put into their hands, and those your Lordship I see has effectually destroyed. It likewise appears that although Greene may himself come to the Northward, his corps is to remain in South Carolina. I therefore suppose your Lordship has recollected this, when you sent orders to Brigadier-general Gould to bring the 19th and 30th regiments to this place, especially as you tell me you still continue in the most painful anxiety for the situation of that province.

I am sorry Lord Rawdon's health should oblige him to return to Europe. I think it is highly proper that either your Lordship, General Leslie, or General O'Hara should go to Charles-town, but I can by no means consent to your Lordship's going thither, before you hear further from me, for very essential reasons which I shall not now trouble your Lordship with.

I am very unhappy to hear of the unfortunate move of our friends and its consequences, as related by Lieutenant Haggarty; those under the influence of Mr. Alexander were desired by me not to rise, and they seemed contented to remain quiet until operation came to them. But it is probable they have no arms to defend themselves; I should imagine that if a station could be found in their neighbourhood, which was safe and tenable, and arms could be given to them, it might be the means of saving many of them: your Lordship will, however, as being upon the spot be the best judge how far this may be proper or practicable, for as I know nothing of the district where this is supposed to have happened, or what their numbers, I cannot say how far it may be expedient to give them assistance. Your Lordship has, I believe, many spare arms in Chesapeak, and there are likewise a considerable number at Charles-town, but if any should be wanted from hence, I will spare as many as I can.

As your Lordship must be sensible how necessary it is I should have frequent and accurate returns of the state of the troops under my command, I am persuaded you will pardon me for requesting you to order that returns are prepared, and, if possible, sent to me every fortnight of the troops under your Lordship's immediate orders in the Chesapeak, and as accurate ones as can be procured of those in Carolina, and the other southern posts.

By the letters brought to me from the Minister by the last packet, I understand that three battalions originally destined for this army, are to accompany Sir George Rodney in case De Grasse comes on this coast, from whence I am to conclude he will be certainly followed by that Admiral. I am likewise told that nearly two thousand two hundred German recruits and auxiliary troops may be hourly expected to arrive here.

I have the honour to be, &c.

H. CLINTON.

Document 3-c†

Cornwallis to Clinton, July, 1781

Cobham 8th July 1781.

Sir, I was this morning honoured with your dispatch of the 28th Ult. The Troops are perfectly ready & will proceed to Portsmouth to wait the Arrival of the Transports; I will give immediate Orders about the Artillery, Stores, &c.

The Transports now at Portsmouth are sufficient to carry the Light Infantry; I had prepared them to receive that Corps, & should have sent them to you in a few days, if your last Order had not arrived. In your cyphered dispatch, the second Battalion of Light Infantry only is mentioned, but I conclude that to be a mistake; & shall keep both ready to embark. I take for granted that General Robertson will come with the Transports to take the command of the Expedition; General Leslie is still here, but as it was not my intention to have sent him with the Troops to New-York, & as he will be the properest person to command, in case you should approve of my returning to Charles-town, I shall not send him on the Expedition unless it shall then

†From: Ibid., pp. 56-59.

appear to be your Excellency's desire, that he should accompany General Robertson.

I must again take the liberty of calling your Excellency's serious attention to the question of the Utility of a defensive post in this Country, which cannot have the smallest influence on the War in Carolina, & which only gives us some Acres of an unhealthy swamp, & is for ever liable to become a prey to a foreign Enemy, with a temporary superiority at Sea. Desultory Expeditions in the Chesapeake, may be undertaken from New-York with as much ease & more safety, whenever there is reason to suppose that our Naval Force is likely to be superior for two or three Months.

The Boats & Naval Assistance having been sent to me by Captain Hudson, I marched on the 4th from Williamsburgh, to a Camp which covered a Ford into the Island of James-Town. The Queen's Rangers passed the River that Evening; on the 5th, I sent over all the Wheel Carriages, & on the 6th the Bat-Horses, & baggage of every kind, intending to pass with the Army on the 7th. About noon on the 6th, information was brought to me of the Approach of the Enemy, and about four in the Afternoon a large Body attacked our Out-posts. Concluding that the Enemy would not bring a considerable Force within our reach, unless they supposed that nothing was left but a rear-guard, I took every means to convince them of my Weakness, & suffered my picquets to be insulted & driven back; nothing, however, appeared near us, but Rifle Men & Militia till near Sun-set, when a Body of Continentals with Artillery began to form in the front of our Camp. I then put the Troops under Arms & ordered the Army to advance in two Lines. The attack was began by the first Line with great spirit; there being nothing but Militia opposed to the Light Infantry, The Action was soon over on the right, but Lieut. Colonel Dundas's Brigade consisting of the 43rd, 76th & 80th Regiments, which formed the left Wing, meeting the Pennsylvania Line, & a detachment of the Marquis de La fayette's Continentals, with two six-pounders, a smart Action ensued for some minutes, when the Enemy gave way, & abandoned their Cannon. The Cavalry were perfectly ready to pursue, but the darkness of the Evening prevented my being able to make use of them. I cannot sufficiently commend the spirit & good behaviour of the Officers & Soldiers of the whole Army; but the 76th & 80th Regiments, on whom the brunt of the Action fell; had an opportunity of distinguishing themselves particularly, & Lieut. Colonel Dundas's Conduct & Gallantry deserve the highest praise. The Force of the Enemy in the Field was about two thousand, & their loss, I believe, between two & three hundred, half an hour more of day-light would probably have given us the greatest part of the Corps. I have inclosed a List of our killed & wounded. We finished our passage yesterday, which has been an operation of great labour & difficulty, as the River is three miles wide at this place; I have great obligations to Captain Aplin & the Officers of the Navy & Seamen, for their great exertions & attention on this occasion.

I have not received the Letters, your Excellency alludes to, of the 29th of May, or 8th & 19th of June.

I have the honour to be, with great respect, Sir, Your most obedient & most humble Servant

CORNWALLIS.

Document 3-d†

Clinton to Cornwallis, July, 1781

Head-Quarters, New-York, July 11, 1781.

My Lord, I am just returned from having a conference with Rear-admiral Graves, in consequence of your Lordship's letter of the 30th ultimo, and we are both clearly of opinion that it is absolutely necessary we should hold a station in Chesapeak for ships of the line, as well as frigates; and the Admiral seems to think that should the enemy possess themselves of Old Point Comfort, Elizabeth River would no longer be of any use to us as a station for the frigates, therefore judges that Hampton-road is the fittest station for all ships, in which your Lordship will see by the papers in your possession, I likewise agree with him. It was moreover my opinion that the possession of York-town, even though we did not possess Gloucester, might give security to the works we might have at Old Point Comfort, which I understand secures Hampton-road.

I had flattered myself that after giving me as nearly three thousand men as you could spare, your Lordship might have had a sufficiency not only to maintain them, but to spare for desultory expeditions; for I had no other plans in view than to draw for the defence of this post, and operation in its neighbourhood, such troops as could be spared from your army, after leaving an ample defensive to such stations as your Lordship might judge proper to occupy; and a small moving corps for desultory water expeditions during the summer months, in which no other might be proper in that unhealthy climate. But as your Lordship seems to think that you can in no degree comply with my requisition for troops, and at the same time establish a post capable of giving protection to ships of war, and it is probable, from what you write me, that you may have repassed James-river and retired to Portsmouth; I beg leave to request that you will without loss of time examine Old Point Comfort, and fortify it; detaining such troops as you may think necessary for that purpose, and garrisoning it afterwards. But if it should be your Lordship's opinion that Old Point Comfort cannot be held without having possession of York, for in this case Gloucester may perhaps be not so material, and that the whole cannot be done with less than seven thousand men, you are at full liberty to detain all the troops now in the Chesapeak, which I believe amount to somewhat more than that number: which very liberal concession will, I am persuaded, convince your Lordship of the high estimation in which I hold a naval station in Chesapeak, especially when you consider that my whole force in this very extensive and important post, is not

†From: Ibid., pp. 62-65.

quite eleven thousand effectives; and how far I may be justifiable in leaving it to so reduced a garrison, time will shew.

I am as much mortified as your Lordship can possibly be at the necessity there is at present for leaving you upon the defensive in Chesapeak; and your Lordship will do me the justice to observe that I have for some months past been myself content with a starved defensive, from the desire I had to give your Lordship as large an army for offensive operations as I could. Therefore, until the season for recommencing operations in the Chesapeak shall return, your Lordship, or whoever remains in the command there, must I fear be content with a strict defensive; and I must desire that you will be pleased to consider this as a positive requisition to you not to detain a greater proportion of the troops now with you than what may be absolutely necessary for defensive operations, &c. as before mentioned. When, therefore, your Lordship has finally determined upon the force you think sufficient for such works as you shall erect at Old Point Comfort, and the number you judge requisite to cover them at York-town, and for the other services of the Chesapeak during the unhealthy season; you will be pleased to send me the remainder. Your Lordship will observe by this that I do not see any great necessity for holding Portsmouth while you have Old Point Comfort: for, should a station on Elizabeth-river be judged necessary, I think Millpoint will answer every necessary purpose of covering frigates, &c. I have the honour to be, &c.

H. CLINTON.

Document 3-e†

Cornwallis to Graves, July, 1781

Portsmouth, July 26, 1781.

Sir, I was honoured with your letter of the 12th of July, by the Solebay, in which you mention a desire of having a harbour secured in the Chesapeak for line of battle ships. I immediately ordered the engineers to examine Old Point Comfort, and went thither myself with the captains of the navy on this station. You will receive a copy of the engineer's report, with a sketch of the peninsula, and the opinion of the officers of the navy relative to the occupying and fortifying of that post.

The Commander-in-chief having signified to me in his letter of the 11th instant, that he thought a secure harbour for line of battle ships of so much importance in the Chesapeak, that he wished me to possess one, even if it should occupy all the force at present in Virginia; and, as it is our unanimous opinion, that Point Comfort will not answer the purpose, I shall immediately sieze and fortify the posts of York and Gloucester, and shall be happy at all times to concur in any measures which may promote the convenience and advantage of his Majesty's navy.

†From: Ibid., p. 100.

I have the honour to be, &c.

CORNWALLIS.

Document 3-f†

Clinton to Cornwallis, August, 1781

New-York, August 11, 1781.

My Lord, I am honoured with your Lordship's dispatches of the 24th and 27th ultimo, which were delivered to me by Captain Stapleton on the 1st instant, which I shall defer answering to a safer opportunity.

I have the pleasure to inform you, that the fleet from Bremer-lehe is this day arrived with two thousand five hundred German recruits.

I hope before this meets your Lordship you will so far have established yourself on the Williamsburg Neck, as to have been able to embark the troops you can spare me for operation here—in which case I have no doubt Captain Hudson will have given every assistance to forward them to us as soon as possible. And if they are not already sailed, I beg that the Queen's Rangers may be the second corps you send me; and that your Lordship will please to recollect my wish to have such a proportion of General Arnold's boats, and artillery men and stores as you can spare. And as you have three engineers, I beg that Lieutenant Sutherland may be sent to this place, as also Captain Fage of the artillery. The French and rebels shewed themselves the other day in front of our lines to the amount of eleven thousand.

A man goes from hence through the country to your Lordship with a proposal to liberate the Convention troops—for which he says he will only want a frigate and some transports to receive them.—Lest any accident should happen to the runner that carries this, a duplicate of it is sent by him in cypher.

H.C.

Document 3-g‡

Cornwallis to Clinton, August, 1781

York-town, Virginia, 22d August, 1781.

Sir, Portsmouth having been completely evacuated without any interruption from the enemy, General O'Hara arrived here this day with the stores and troops; and a great number of refugees have accompanied him from the counties of Norfolk, Suffolk, and Princess Anne.

The engineer has finished his survey and examination of this place, and has proposed his plan for fortifying it; which appearing judicious, I have approved of, and directed to be executed.

†From: Ibid., pp. 123-24.
‡From: Ibid., pp. 137-39.

The works at Gloucester are now in such forwardness, that a smaller detachment than the present garrison would be in safety against a sudden attack; but I make no alteration there, as I cannot hope that the labour of the whole will complete that post in less than five or six weeks.

My experience there of the fatigue and difficulty of constructing works in this warm season, convinces me, that all the labour that the troops here will be capable of, without ruining their health, will be required at least for six weeks to put the intended works at this place in a tolerable state of defence. And as your Excellency has been pleased to communicate to me your intention of re-commencing operations in the Chesapeak about the beginning of October, I will not venture to take any step that might retard the establishing of this post: but I request that your Excellency will be pleased to decide whether it is more important for your plans that a detachment of a thousand or twelve hundred men, which I think I can spare from every other purpose but that of labour, should be sent to you from hence, or that the whole of the troops here should be employed in expediting the works.

My last accounts of the enemy were, that the Marquis de la Fayette was encamped in the fork of the Pamunky and Matapony with his own detachment of Continentals, a considerable body of eighteen-months men, and two brigades of militia under Stevens and Lawson; that he had armed four hundred of the seven hundred Virginia prisoners lately arrived from Charles-town, and expected to be joined in a short time by General Smallwood with seven hundred eighteen-months men from Maryland; and that Generals Wayne and Morgan having returned from the other side of James river, were likewise on their march to join him.

There being only four eighteens and one twenty-four pounder here, more heavy guns will be wanted for the sea batteries at this place, and we are likewise in want of many other artillery and engineer's stores, the returns of which I take the liberty to inclose.

It is proper to mention to your Excellency, that you may make your arrangements accordingly, that there are only about six hundred stand of spare arms in the Chesapeak; and that our consumption of provisions is considerably increased by a number of refugees lately come to us, and by negroes that are employed in different branches of the public service.

I have the honour to be, &c.

CORNWALLIS.

4

America's Alternatives: New York or Virginia?

Document 4-a†

Washington to Lafayette, July, 1780

[Hd. Qrs., Prekeniss, July 27, 1780.]

I have received your letter of the 22d. from Hartford. I perceive my Dear Marquis, you are determined, at all events to take New York, and that obstacles only increase your zeal. I am sorry our prospects instead of brightening grow duller. I have already written to you on the subject of arms. There is no probability of our getting the number we want from the states, so that without the timely arrival of those we expect, or the assistance of our allies, this alone will prove an insuperable obstacle. Our levies come in even slower than I expected; though we have still abundance of fair promises, and some earnest of performance from the Eastern states. Pensylvania has given us not quite four hundred, and seems to think she has done admirably. Jersey has given fifty or sixty; but I do not despair of Jersey.

Mr. Clinton still continues to threaten your country men with a combined attack. You will judge as well as me of the probability of his being sincere; but I have put the troops here under marching orders, and have ordered those at West Point to Kings ferry.

If Clinton moves in force to Rhode Island we may possibly be able to take advantage of it, or we may embarrass him a little and precipitate his movements. In this case there are only two things that would hinder us from taking New York before you return; the want of men and arms to do it with.

If this letter should not meet you on your way back, a visit from you to the Council of Massachusetts may have a good effect. Urge the absolute necessity of giving us their full complement of men, and of doing every thing else that has been asked of them. Dwell upon the articles of arms and ammunition. With the truest Affection etc.

†From: Fitzpatrick, ed., *The Writing of George Washington*, vol. 19, pp. 269-70.

Document 4-b†

Conference at Wethersfield, May, 1781

Wethersfield, May 23, 1781.

Rochambeau: The project to transport the entire French army to Chesapeake Bay in Barras' squadron.

1st. Washington: However desirable such an event might have been, the reasons now assigned to the Count de Barras are sufficient to prove its impracticability.

Rochambeau: Should the French army march to the North River what position should Barras' squadron take?

2d. Washington: It is Genl. Washington's opinion that the Plan of Campaign will render it necessary for the French Army to march from Newport towards the North River as soon as possible and that consequently it will be advisable for the Count de Barras (agreeable to his instructions in that case provided) to seek the first favorable moment of removing the Squadron under his command to Boston.

Rochambeau: In such case, what arrangements are to be made to hold Rhode Island?

3d. Washington: As the harbor of Rhode Island may be useful to the Fleets of his most Christian Majesty, it is Genl. Washington's opinion, that a force should be left for the security of Newport, but as the Enemy will not be in condition from the present circumstances of their affairs, to detach any considerable body of Men to re-possess the Island, it has been agreed upon between His Excellency Count de Rochambeau and Genl. Washington, that 500 Militia, under a good Officer, will be sufficient for the Guards for the Works. but in case of an enterprize against them, a greater force should be called for their defence.

Rochambeau: If Rhode Island be evacuated what disposition should be made of the heavy artillery and stores that are too heavy to move easily?

4th. Washington: In the former communications between His Excellency Count de Rochambeau and Genl. Washington, it was understood that the French Fleet was to have remained in the harbor of Newport after the removal of the Army, and therefore, Providence was fixed upon as a safe and proper deposit of the heavy Artillery and Spare Stores. It now being determined that the Fleet shall embrace the first oppertunity of going round to the Harbour of Boston it is to be wished that the heavy Artillery and spare Stores should be sent round also. But Genl. Washington being informed by His Excellency Count de Rochambeau that they have been already deposited at Providence, and that it will be impossible under the present circumstances of the Fleet and want of Transportation to remove them to Boston he is of opinion that they may safely remain there under the Guard of 200 French Troops, who will be aided by the Militia of the Country in case of Need. The possession of Newport will add to their security.

†From: Ibid., vol. 22, pp. 105-7.

Rochambeau: In event of a French naval reenforcement from the West Indies, what operations will be undertaken by the combined allied forces?

5th. Washington: The Enemy by several detachments from New York having reduced their force at that Post to less than one half of the number which they had at the time of the former conference at Hartford in September last; it is thought advisable to form a junction of the French and American Armies upon the North River as soon as possible, and move down to the vicinity of New York to be ready to take advantage of any oppertunity which the weakness of the enemy may afford. Should the West India Fleet arrive upon the Coast; the force thus combined may either proceed in the operation against New Yk. or may be directed against the enemy in some other quarter, as circumstances shall dictate. The great waste of Men (which we have found from experience) in the long Marches to the Southern States; the advanced season now, to commence these in, and the difficulties and expence of Land transportation thither, with other considerations too well known to His Excellency Count de Rochambeau to need detailing, point out the preference which an operation against New York seems to have, in present circumstances, to attempt sending a force to the Southward.

Answer to the P.S. The observation upon the 4th. head sufficiently answers this, as the 500 Militia proposed to be Stationed at Newport may be disposed of in any manner which His Excellency Count de Rochambeau may think proper.

Document 4-c†

Washington to Rochambeau, June, 1781

Head Quarters, New Windsor, June 4, 1781.

Sir: I had last Evening the honor of receiving your favor of the 31st. of May by the Duke de Lauzun, who informs me that he is authorized by your Excellency and the Count de Barras to enter into a free communication with me upon the subject of the Council of War held on board the Duke de Burgoyne and to request my opinion upon the propriety of their determination.

I must confess to your Excellency that there is weight in the reasons which are offered for the detention of His Majesty's Fleet in the Harbour of Newport in preference to its going round to Boston, but as I cannot think that it will be as safe in all possible cases in the Harbour of Newport, after the greater part of the French Army has been withdrawn, as it would be in the Harbour of Boston, I must adhere to my *opinion* and to the plan which was fixed at Weathersfield as most eligible, all circumstances considered. I would not however set up my single judgment against that of so many Gentlemen of experience, more especially as the matter partly depends upon a knowledge of Marine Affairs of which I candidly confess my ignorance. I would therefore [in order to avoid delay] rest the matter upon the following

†From: Ibid., pp. 156-58.

footing. If your Excellency, the Count De Barras, and the other Gentlemen should upon a further consideration of the subject, aided by any new informations which you may have received, still think it most advisable to adhere to the former resolution of the Council, you may make use of the inclosed letters to the Governors of Massachusetts and Rhode Island, which are left open for your inspection. If on the contrary you should change your opinions the letters may be destroyed, as that which was written by me to the Governor of Rhode Island from Weathersfield will be sufficient for the purpose of calling out 500 Militia for the present and such further numbers as exigencies may require.

At any rate I could wish that the march of the troops might now be hurried as much as possible. The strides which the Enemy are making to the southward demand a collection of our force in this quarter, that we may endeavour to commence our operations. I know of no measure which will be so likely to afford relief to the southern States in so short a time as a serious menace against New York. This your Excellency may remember was a principal inducement for our undertaking that operation in preference to the other which was spoken of, and I assure you the calls upon me from the southward are so pressing that nothing but seeing our preparations against New York in some degree of forwardness will content them or convince them that they are likely to derive any advantages from the force which they see detained here.

I have forwarded your Excellency's dispatch to the Minister by a Gentleman in the Quarter Masters department. I have the honor etc.

Document 4-d†

Washington to Luzerne, May, 1781

Wethersfield, May 23, 1781.

Sir: The letter which I have the honor to inclose from the Count de Rochambeau will, I imagine, inform your Excellency of the intended march of the French army towards the North River, and of the destination of the Kings Squadron now in the harbour of Newport, (if circumstances will admit of the respective movements). I should be wanting in respect and confidence were I not to add, that our object is new York. The Season, the difficulty and expence of Land transportation, and the continual waste of men in every attempt to reinforce the Southern States, are almost insuperable objections to marching another detachment from the Army on the North River; nor do I see how it is possible to give effectual support to those States, and avert the evils which threaten them, while we are inferior in naval force in these Seas. It is not for me to know in what manner the Fleet of His Most Christian Majesty is to be employed in the W. Indies this Summer or to enquire at what epocha it may be expected on this Coast; but the appearance and aid of it in this Quarter is of such essential importance in any offensive operation, and so necessary to stop the progress of the enemys arms to the Southward, that I

†From: Ibid., pp. 103-4.

shall be excused, I am perswaded, for endeavouring to engage your Excellencys good offices in facilitating an event on which so much depends. For this I have a stronger plea when I assure you, that General Rochambeau's opinion and wishes concur with mine and that it is at his instance principally I make you this address.

If we are happy enough to find your Excellency in sentiment with us, it will be in your power to inform the Count de Grasse of the strength and situation of the enemys Naval and land force in this Country, the destination of the French Squadron under Admiral Barras and the intention of the Allied arms if a junction can be formed. at present the B. Fleet lyes within Block Island and about five leagues from Point Judith.

The Count de Rochambeau and the Chevr. Chartellux agree perfectly in Sentiment with me, that while affrs. remain as they now are, the West India Fleet should run immediately to Sandy hook, [if there are no concerted operations] where it may be met with all the information requisite, and where, most likely, it will shut in, or cut off, Adml. Arbuthnot; and may be joined by the Count de Barras. An early and frequent communication from the Count de Grasse, would lead to preparatory measures on our part, and be a means of facilitating the operation in hand, or any other which may be thought more advisable.

I know your Excellency's goodness, and your zeal for the common cause too well, to offer any thing more as an apology for this liberty; and I perswade myself it is unnecessary for me to declare the respect and attachment with which etc.

Document 4-e†

Rochambeau to de Grasse, June, 1781

From Providence, the 11th of June, 1781.

I have received, Sir, by the hand of M. de Moulue (?), who arrived only yesterday in Boston, with a part of his convoy, a third of it having been dispersed by a wind storm, the letter which you honored me by writing on the 29th of March. ... As for what concerns me, I am attaching herewith a duplicate of the letter which I had the honor of writing you on the 28th and 31st of May. Since that time I have received four letters from General Washington urging me to march on the River of the North [Hudson] which he regards militarily and politically, under the present circumstances, as absolutely necessary and urgent. The second council of war which he had ordered, on the safety of the squadron, was held the 8th and I left on the 10th to come here where I am going to gather as many recruits as I can from the convoy, (with) the money, and leave in 5 or 6 days to go and join the General, and try by threatening New York with him to create a diversion for the benefit of Virginia. I must not conceal from you, Sir, that these people are at the end of ... their means, that Washington will not have half of the

†From: Manuscript in French at the Library of Congress. Translated by William A. Henning.

troops he counted on having, and that I believe, though he is keeping this secret that he does not at present have 6,000 men, that M. de Lafayette does not have 1,000 regulars along with the militia to defend Virginia, and about as many are en route to join him, that General Greene has attacked Camden where he was repulsed, and that I don't know when and how he will join M. de Lafayette, that it is therefore of the utmost importance that you take on board as many troops as you can, that 4 or 5 thousand men would not be too many, either to help us to destroy their establishments in Portsmouth in Virginia near Hampton Roads, where until now they have always kept 1,500 men while the others operate in the countryside, and all their flotillas with which they go out in the rivers to harass poor M. de Lafayette in a most unfortunate manner; or then to force the Hook by seizing Sandyhook with your land troops which should facilitate the entry of this harbor for your squadron. We are sure that the *Sandwich* entered and left in September and more recently the *London*. Finally, to help us afterward to lay siege to Brooklyn, assuming that we would be able to establish ourselves with 8,000 men on this point of Long Island, and to keep 5 or 6 thousand on the River of the North to cut off King Bridge. There, Sir, are the different objectives which you could have in view, and the present, unpleasant picture of affairs in this country.

I am quite confident that you will bring us maritime superiority, but I cannot repeat too often that you should also bring troops and money. I had the honor of writing you a personal letter on this last matter, of which I am again enclosing herewith a duplicate. In addition, I have the honor of repeating, Sir, that it is indispensable that General Washington and M. de Barras be notified by frigate of the time of your arrival and the place of your landing.

I have the honor of being, &c. le Comte de Rochambeau

Document 4-f†

Washington to Rochambeau. June, 1781

Head Quarters, New Windsor, June 13, 1781.

Sir: I am honored by your Excellency's favors of the 9th. and 10th: instants; and with their very interesting communications which you may be assured will be kept perfectly secret. I flatter myself that the whole Convoy will arrive in safety in some of the Eastern ports, as I believe the British ships are all cruising off the Hook.

The Count De Barras has furnished me with the Result of the second Council of War. I have so high a respect for the opinions of the Gentlemen who composed it, that I should have been satisfied had they barely mentioned their adherence to their former determination, but the new arguments which have been introduced in favor of the detention of the *Fleet* at *Rhode Island* leaves me no room to doubt of the propriety of the measure.

†From: Fitzpatrick, ed., *The Writings of George Washington*, vol. 22, pp. 207-9.

I am so fully convinced that your Excellency will make no unnecessary delay in your march, that I have only occasion to repeat my former request, that it may be commenced as soon as circumstances will admit. My last accounts from the Marquis de la Fayette were of the 3d. of June. The British Army, in very considerable force, were then between Richmond and Fredericksburg; their destination was uncertain, but from their superiority they were at full liberty to go wherever they pleased. The inclosed Copy of a letter from the president of Congress to me will give your Excellency the latest intelligence from South Carolina.

Your requisitions to the *Count De Grasse*, go to every thing I could wish. You cannot, in my opinion, too strongly urge the necessity of bringing a *Body of Troops* with him, more especially, as I am very dubious whether our force can be drawn together by the time he proposes to be here. Now *4000* or *5000 Men* in addition to what we shall certainly have by that time, would almost beyond a doubt, enable us, with the assistance of the *Fleet* to carry our object. It is to be regretted that the *Counts* stay upon this *Coast* will be limited. That consideration is an additional reason for wishing a force equal to giving a speedy determination to the operation.

Your Excellency will be pleased to recollect that *New York* was looked upon by us as the only practicable object under present circumstances; but should we be able to secure a *naval superiority*, we may perhaps find others more practicable and equally advisable. If the *Frigate* should not have sailed, I wish you to explain this matter to the *Count de Grasse*, as, if I understand you, you have in your communication to him, confined our views to *New York* alone. And instead of advising him to run immediately into *Chesapeak*, will it not be best to leave him to judge, from the information he may from time to time receive of the situation of the *enemy's Fleet* upon this *Coast*, which will be the most advantageous quarter for him to make his *appearance* in. In the letter which was written to the Minister from Weathersfield, in which he was requested to urge the *Count* to come this way with his *whole Fleet, Sandy Hook* was mentioned as the most desirable point. Because, by coming suddenly there he would certainly *block* up any *fleet* which might be *within*; and he would even have a very good chance of *forcing* the *entrance* before dispositions could be made to *oppose* him. Should the *British Fleet* not be there, he could follow them to *Chesapeak*, which is always accessible to a superior force. I have the Honor &c.

Document 4-g†

Entries from Washington's Diaries, July, 1781

15th. The Savage Sloop of War of 16 Guns—the ship Genl. Washington, lately taken by the Enemy—a ten gun Galley and two other small armed Vessels passed our post at Dobbs Ferry (which was not in a condition to

†From: John C. Fitzpatrick, ed., *George Washington's Diaries*, 4 vols. (Boston: Houghton Mifflin Co., 1925), vol. 2, pp. 236-39.

oppose them)—at the same time three or four River Vessels with 4 Eighteen pounders, Stores &ca. had just arrived at Tarrytown and with infinite difficulty, and by great exertion of Colo. Sheldon, Captn. Hurlbut, (who got wounded)—Captn. Lieutt. Miles of the Artillery and Lt. Shayler were prevented falling into the hands of the Enemy as they got a ground 100 yards from the Dock and were set fire to by the Enemy but extinguished by the extraordinary activity and spirit of the above Gentl.—two of the Carriages however were a good deal damaged by the fire. The Enemy however by sending their armed Boats up the River took the Vessel of a Captn. Dobbs laden with Bread for the French Army—cloathing for Sheldons Regiment and some passengers. This was done in the Night—it being after Sunset before the Vessels passed the Post at Dobbs ferry.

16th. The Cannon and Stores were got out of the Vessels and every thing being removed from Tarrytown, two french twelve pounders, and one of our 18 prs. were brought to bear upon the Ships which lay of Tarrytown, distant about a Mile, and obliged them to remove lower down and more over to the West shore.

17th. The Vessels being again fired at in the position they took yesterday run up the River to Tellers point and there come to burning the House of the Widow Noyell.

18th. I passed the North River with Count de Rochambeau—Genl. de Beville his Qr: Mr. Genl. and Genl. Duportail in order to Reconnoitre the Enemy Posts and Encampments at the North end of York Island—took an Escort of 150 Men from the Jersey Troops on the other side.

From different views the following discoveries were made—viz—

That two Ships of 20 Guns and upwards lay opposite to the Mouth of Spikendevil—one pretty near the East Shore the other abt the same distance from the West; the first is intended to guard the Mouth of Spikendevil equally with the No. River. Below there, and directly opposite to Fort Washington (or Knyphausen) lay two transports with about 6 Guns and few men in each, the Easternmost Ship seems to designed to Guard the landing at the little bay above Jefferys Rock. About the center of the Ground leading to Jefferys Rock or point a Guard Mounts. It appears to be no more than a Sergeants guard with one Centry in front where there is a small Work—the Guard House standing within.

These are all the Guards and all the security I could discover upon the No. River on the Right flank of the Enemy—the shore from Jeffreys Rock downwards, was quite open, and free—without Hutts of any kind—Houses or Troops—none being encamped below the heights. There did not even appear springs, or washing places anywhere on the face of the Hill which were resorted to.

The Island is totally stripped of Trees, and wood of every kind; but low bushes (apparently as high as a Man's Waste) appear in places which were covered with wood in the year 1776.

The side of the Hill from the Barrier below Fort Tryon, to the Bay opposite to fort Knyphausen, is difficult of access; but there seems to be a place abt. 200 yds. above the bay, which has the best appearance of landing, and is most private—but a hut or two on the heights abt. 200 yds. above Fort Knyphausen, and a little above the old long Battery, which was thrown up in 1776 must be avoided by leaving it on the left in getting to the Fort last mentioned.

In the hollow below Morris's heights (between that and Haerlam) is a good place to land, but near the York Road opposite there appeared to be a few Tents and many Dragoon Horses seemed to be at Pasture in the low land between the heights. A landing perfectly concealed, but not so good, might be made a little higher up the River, and nearer to those heights which ought to be immediately occupied (between the old American lines and the aforesaid hollow).

From the point within the Mouth of Spikendevil, the way to the Fort on Cox's Hill seems difficult, and the first part of it covered with bushes—there is a better way up from the outer point, but too much exposed to a discovery from the Ship which lays opposite to it and on acct. of its being less covered with wood.

The ground around the Fort on Cox's Hill is clear of Bushes—there is an abatis round the Work, but no friezing; nor could I discover whether there is a ditch. At the No. Et. corner there appeared to be no Parapet and the whole seemed to be in a decaying State—the gate is next the No. River.

Forts Tryon and Knyphausen and Ft. George or Laurell, with the Batteries in the line of Pallisading across from River to River appeared to be well friezed, ditched and abbatied. In a word to be strong and in good repair.

Fort N. 8. is also abatied and friezed at the Top—the gate is next Haerlam River—there are no Houses or Huts on the side of the Hill from this work till you come near old Fort Independence.

On McGowans heights there appears (by the extent of the Tents) to be two Battns. Encamped—supposed to be the British Grenadiers—a little in the rear of this, and on the (enemys) left, are a number of Huts—but whether they are inhabited or not could not be ascertained—there being different opinions on this point, from the nearest view we could get of it. On the height opposite to Morris' white House there appeared to be another Regt. (supposed to be the 38th British). Between this and Fort Knyphausen (abt. half way) are two small Encampments contiguous to each other—both together containing two or 3 and 40 Tents.— Hessians—on Laurel Hill near Fort George is another Encampment in view abt. 40 Tents and huts which appear to be Inhabited also by (it is said) the 57th Regiment. The other and only remaining encampment in View, and discoverable from the West side of the River, is betwn. the Barrier and Kingsbridge—in the hollow between Cox's hill and the heights below—one hundred Tents could be counted in view at the same time, and others Might be hid by the Hills—at this place it is said the Jagers—Hessian and Anspach lay.

Document 4-h†

Washington to de Grasse, July, 1781

Head Quarters, Dobbs's Ferry, July 21, 1781.

Sir: Your Excellency will have been informed by the Chevr. de la Luzerne of the ardent wishes of these United States to see the Fleet under your command in these Seas; will have been told the advantages which would in all probability be the result of such a movement; how essential it would be to make an early communication of your approach, and that you would be met off *Sandy Hook* with such details as might be necessary for your Government.

In full confidence that you will be soon upon this Coast, I have the honor to inform you that the allied Armies have formed a junction and taken a position about ten Miles above the enemy's posts on the North end of York Island. Their Right at Dobb's Ferry on the North or Hudson's River, their left extending to a small River called the Brunx. The French Force consists of about *4400* Men. The American is at this time but *small*, but expected to be *considerably augmented.* In this however we may be disappointed. And as the time of your arrival and the succour you may bring are altogether uncertain no definitive plan of operation has been or can be fixed. It must depend upon the situation of the enemy at the moment of your approach, and upon the force we shall be able to oppose to them in any given point.

The Enemy's land force in *New York* and *its dependencies*, including some late reinforcements from England, may amount at this time to about *5000* Regular Troops besides Militia, which may be about *3000* more. but they may be reinforced from Virginia, and the event is expected, unless they should be prevented by the arrival of your Excellency upon the Coast or some other intervention. Should they be hindered from effecting a further junction of Force at New York, that City and its dependencies are our primary objects. Your Excellency, by being in possession of the Harbour within Sandy Hook, would give facility if not certainty to the operation, but the practicability of gaining the entrance will be with your Excellency to determine, upon your general knowledge of the place, from your own observation upon the spot, and upon the information you will receive from the Pilots who accompany you.

The Enemy's naval force at New York consists at present of only six Ships of the Line. I think two of 50 Guns and a few Frigates. The Royal Oak, a ship of the line, has lately been sent to Halifax to receive some repairs which could not be done at New York.

The second object, in case we should find our force and means incompetent to the first, is the relief of Virginia, or such of the southern States as the enemy may be found in, by transporting the principal part of

†From: Fitzpatrick, ed., *The Writings of George Washington*, vol. 22, pp. 400-2.

our force suddenly to that quarter; and that we may be ready for such an event, preparations are making to facilitate such a movement. But of this I hope there will be no occasion, as I flatter myself the glory of destroying the British Squadron at New York is reserved for the Kings Fleet under your command, and that of the land Force at the same place for the allied Arms.

A Gentleman of the name of Forman, who will probably have the honor of delivering this to you, is a person in whom you may perfectly confide and who will forward your dispatches immediately to me.

If you are not sufficiently provided with pilots, some of the most expert and trusty shall be sent to you without delay. I have the honor etc.

5

The Decision for Virginia

Document 5-a†

Washington to Lafayette, July, 1781

Head Quarters near Dobbs's ferry, July 30, 1781.
My dear Marquis: I take your private letter of the 20th. of this Month in the light which you wish it; that of an unreserved Communication from one Friend to another; and I should be wanting in Candor were I not to expose my sentiments to you in as free a manner.

I am convinced that your desire to be with this Army arises principally from a wish to be actively useful. You will not therefore regret your stay in Virginia untill matters are reduced to a greater degree of certainty than they are at present, especially when I tell you, that, from the change of circumstances with which the removal of part of the Enemy's force from Virginia to New York will be attended, it is more than probable that we shall also intirely change our plan of operations. I think we have already effected one part of the plan of Campaign settled at Weathersfield, that is, giving a substantial relief to the southern States by obliging the enemy to recall a considerable part of their force from thence. Our views must now be turned towards endeavouring to expel them totally from those States, [if we find ourselves incompt. to the seige of N.Y.] The difficulty of doing this does not so much depend upon obtaining a force capable of effecting it, as upon the mode of collecting that force to the proper point, and transporting the provisions, Stores &c. necessary for such an operation. You are fully acquainted with the almost impracticability of doing this by land; to say nothing of the amazing loss of Men always occasioned by long marches, and those towards a quarter in which the service is disagreeable. I should not however hesitate in encountering these difficulties great as they are, had we not prospects of transporting ourselves in a manner safe, easy and expeditious. Your penetration will point out my meaning, which I cannot venture to express in direct terms.

I approve your resolution to reinforce General Greene in proportion to the detachment which the enemy may make to New York. Let your next attention be paid to training and forming the Militia with which you may be furnished and disposing of them in such a manner that they may be drawn at the shortest notice to whatever point the enemy make their capital post, and which I conclude will be at portsmouth. The establishment of Magazines at safe deposits will be in all cases necessary; but above all things I recommend

†From: Ibid., vol. 22, pp. 432-34.

an augmentation of your Cavalry to as great a height as possible. It may happen that the enemy may be drove to the necessity of forcing their way thro' North Carolina to avoid a greater misfortune. A superiority of Horse upon our side would be fatal to them in such a case.

The advantages resulting from a move of the French Fleet from Newport to Chesapeak were early and strongly pointed out to Count de Barras and I thought he had once agreed to put it into execution, but by his late letters, he seem'd to think that such a maneuvre might interfere with greater plans and therefore he declined it. It would now be too late to answer the principal object, as by accounts from a deserter, the troops arrived from Virginia last Friday.

Should your Return to this Army be finally determined, I cannot flatter you with a command equal to your expectations or my wishes. You know the over proportion of General Officers to our numbers and can therefore conceive where the difficulty will lie. General Mcdougal is not yet provided for and the Jersey and York troops are reserved for him, [they are promis'd to him tho'] they have not yet joined.

In my letter to General Greene, which I beg the favor of you to forward, I have hinted nothing of what I have said to you, for fear of a miscarriage. You will probably find a safe opportunity from your Army to him and you will oblige me by communicating the part of this letter which relates to my [expectation] of being able to transport part of this Army to the southward, should the operation against New York be declined.

I wish, as I mentioned in my last, to send a confidential person to you to explain at large what I have so distantly hinted, but I am really at a loss [for want of knowing the Officr better], to find one upon whose discretion I can depend. My own family you know are constantly and fully employed. I however hope I have spoken plain enough to be understood by you. [With every sentimt. of Affectn.] etc.

Document 5-b†

Entries from Washington's Diaries, August, 1781

August *1st.* By this date all my Boats were ready, viz—one hundred New ones at Albany (constructed under the direction of Genel. Schuyler) and the like number at Wappings Creek by the Qr. Mr. Genl.; besides old ones which have been repaired. My heavy Ordnance and Stores from the Eastward had also come on to the North Rivr. and every thing would have been in perfect readiness to commence the operation against New York, if the States had furnished their quotas of men agreeably to my requisitions; but so far have they been from complying with these that of the first not more than half the number asked of them have joined the Army and of 6200 of the latter

---

†From: John C. Fitzpatrick, ed., *George Washington's Diaries* (Boston: Houghton Mifflin Co., 1925), vol. 2, pp. 248-50.

pointedly and continuously called for to be with the army by the 15th of last Month, only 176 had arrived from Connecticut, independant of abt. 300 State Troops under the Command of Genl. Waterbury, which had been on the lines before we took the field, and two Companies of York levies (abt. 80 Man) under similar circumstances.

Thus circumstanced, and having little more than general assurances of getting the succours called for and energetic Laws and Resolves energetically executed, to depend upon, with little appearance of their fulfilment, I could scarce see a ground upon wch. to continue my preparations against New York; especially as there was much reason to believe that part (at least) of the Troops in Virginia were recalled to reinforce New York and therefore I turned my views more seriously (than I had before done) to an operation to the Southward and, in consequence, sent to make inquiry, indirectly, of the principal Merchants to the Eastward what number, and what time, Transports could be provided to convey a force to the Southward if it should be found necessary to change our plan and similar application was made in a direct way to Mr. Morris (Financier) to discover what number cd. be had by the 20th. of this month at Philadelphia, or in Chesapeak bay. At the same time General Knox was requested to turn his thoughts to this business and make every necessary arrangement for it in his own mind, estimating the ordnance and Stores which would be wanting and how many of them could be obtained without a transport of them from the North River. Measures were also taken to deposit the Salt provisions in such places as to be Water born, more than these, while there remained a hope of Count de Grasse's bringing a land force with him, and that the States might yet put us in circumstances to prosecute the original plan could not be done without unfolding matters too plainly to the enemy and enabling them thereby to counteract our Schemes.

4th. Fresh representations of the defenceless State of the Northern frontier, for want of the Militia so longed called for, and expected from Massachusetts bay, accompanied by a strong expression of the fears of the People that they should be under the necessity of abandoning that part of the Country and an application that the Second York Regiment (Courtlandts) at *least* should be left for their protection induced me to send Major Genl. Lincoln (whose influence in his own State was great) into the Counties of Berkshire and Hampshire to enquire into the causes of these delays and to hasten on the Militia. I wrote at the same time to the Governor of this State consenting to suffer the 4 Companies of Courtlandts Regiment (now at Albany) to remain in that Quarter till the Militia did come in, but observed that if the States instead of filling their Battalions and sending forth their Militia were to be calling upon, and expecting me to dissipate the sml. operating force under my command for local defences that all offensive operations must be relinquished and we must content ourselves (in case of compliance) to spend an inactive and injurious Campaign which might, at this critical moment, be ruinous to the common cause of America.

Document 5-c†

De Grasse to Washington, [Haiti] July 28, 1781

... I have seen with regret the distress, which prevails on the continent, and the necessity of the prompt succours you solicit. I have conferred with M. de Lillancourt, who took command of the government here on the day of my arrival, and engaged him to furnish from the garrison of St. Domingo a detachment from the regiments of Gatinois, Agenois, and Tourraine, amounting in all to three thousand men, one hundred artillery, one hundred dragoons, ten pieces of field ordnance, and several of siege artillery and mortars. The whole will be embarked in vessels of war, from twenty-five to twenty-nine in number, which will depart from this colony on the 3d of August, and proceed directly to the Chesapeake Bay, which place seems to be indicated by yourself, General Washington, M. de la Luzerne, and Count de Barras, as the best point of operation for accomplishing the object proposed.

I have likewise done all in my power to procure for you the sum of twelve hundred thousand livres, which you say is absolutely necessary. This colony is not in a condition to afford you such a supply; but I shall obtain it from Havana, whither a frigate will be sent for the purpose, and you may depend on receiving that amount.

As neither myself, nor the troops commanded by the Marquis de St. Simon, can remain on the continent after the 15th of October, I shall be greatly obliged to you if you will employ me promptly and effectually within that time, whether against the maritime or land forces of our enemy. It will not be possible for me to leave the troops with you beyond that period; first, because part of them are under the orders of the Spanish generals, and have been obtained only on the promise, that they shall be returned by the time they will be wanted; and, secondly, because the other part are destined to the garrison of St. Domingo, and cannot be spared from that duty by M. de Lillancourt. The entire expedition, in regard to these troops, has been concerted only in consequence of your request, without even the previous knowledge of the ministers of France and Spain. I have thought myself authorized to assume this responsibility for the common cause; but I should not dare so far to change the plans they have adopted, as to remove so considerable a body of troops.

You clearly perceive the necessity of making the best use of the time, that will remain for action. I hope the frigate, which takes this letter, will have such despatch, that everything may be got in readiness by the time of my arrival, and that we may proceed immediately to fulfill the designs in view, the success of which I ardently desire.

---

†From: H.L. Landers, *The Virginia Campaign and the Blockade and Siege of Yorktown, 1781* (Washington, D.C.: Government Printing Office, 1931), pp. 155-57.

Document 5-d†

Entries from Washington's Diaries, August, 1781

14th. Received dispatches from the Count de Barras announcing the intended departure of the Count de Grasse from cape Francois with between 25 and 29 Sail of the line and 3200 land Troops on the 3d. Instant for Chesapeak bay and the anxiety of the latter to have every thing in the most perfect readiness to commence our operations in the moment of his arrival as he should be under a necessity from particular engagements with the Spaniards to be in the West Indies by the Middle of October, at the same time intimating his (Barras's) Intentions of enterprizing something against Newfoundland, and against which both Genl. Rochambeau and myself Remonstrated as impolitic and dangerous under the probability of Rodneys coming up this Coast.

Matters having now come to a crisis and a decisive plan to be determined on, I was obliged, from the shortness of Count de Grasses, promised stay on this Coast, the apparent disinclination in their Naval Officers to force the harbour of New York and the feeble compliance of the States to my requisitions for Men, hitherto, and little prospect of greater exertion in the future, to give up all idea of attacking New York; and instead thereof to remove the French Troops and a detachment from the American Army to the Head of Elk to be transported to Virginia for the purpose of co-operating with the force from the West Indies against the Troops in that State.

Document 5-e‡

Washington to de Grasse, August, 1781

Camp at Phillipsbg., August 17, 1781.

Sir: In consequence of the dispatches received from your Excellency by the Frigate La Concorde it has been judged expedient to give up for the present the enterprise against New York and to turn our attention towards the South, with a view, if we should not be able to attempt Charles town itself, to recover and secure the States of Virginia, North Carolina and the Country of South Carolina and Georgia. We may add a further inducement for giving up the first mentioned enterprise, which is the arrival of a reinforcement of near 3000 Hessian Recruits. For this purpose we have determined to remove the whole of the French Army and as large a detachment of the American as can be spared, to Chesapeak, to meet Your Exlency there.

The following appear to us the principal Cases which will present themselves, and upon which we shall be obliged ultimately to form our plans. We have therefore stated them, with a few short observations upon each. Your Excellency will be pleased to revolve them in your own mind and

†From: John C. Fitzpatrick, ed., *George Washington's Diaries* (Boston: Houghton Mifflin Co., 1925), vol. 2, pp. 253-54.

‡From: Fitzpatrick, ed., *Writings of George Washington*, vol. 23, pp. 6-11.

prepare your own opinion by the time we shall have the pleasure of meeting you in Virginia.

1st. What shall be done if the Enemy should be found with the greater part of their force in Virginia upon the arrival of the French Fleet?

2d. Should only a detachment be found there?

3d. Should the British force be totally withdrawn from thence?

Upon the first, it appears to us that we ought, without loss of time, to attack the enemy with our United Force.

Upon the second, it appears proper to destine such part of our force as will be amply sufficient to reduce the enemys detachment, and then determine what use shall be made of the remainder; and here two things present themselves for our consideration. The enemy will either have sent the greater part of their force, from Virginia, to New York or to Charles town. If to New York, (which is the least probable under present circumstances) Charles town will have but a moderate Garrison and it may be possible to attack it to advantage. If to Charles town, Then the Enemy will be so superior to General Greene, that they will be able to regain the whole of the State of south Carolina and of consequence, Georgia. We therefore think that in this last case such a force at least should be detached to South Carolina as will enable us to keep the field and confine the enemy in or near to Charles town.

In the third case which we stated, we mean that of supposing the enemy should have totally evacuated Virginia. It appears to us necessary to make a solid establishment at portsmouth, or any other place if more proper, in order to render a Fleet in Chesapeak Bay entirely secure, and to employ the remainder of our land force and such Vessels as may be proper for the service as has been explained in the preceding Article. That is, either in the seige of Charles town, if the Garrison shall be found sufficiently weak to warrant the attempt, or to cover and secure the Country should it be found otherwise.

Returning back to the enterprise agt. New York will depend upon a number of circumstances, the discussion of which we will leave untill we have the happiness of a conference with your Excellency. We have only to observe that the execution of all or any of the plans which we have proposed, go upon a supposition of a decided Naval superiority; except that of marching a reinforcement into south Carolina.

We would beg leave to take up so much of your Excellency's time, as to point out to you the vast importance of Charles town and what advantages the enemy derive from the possession of it. It is the Centre of their power in the south. By holding it, they preserve a dangerous influence throughout the whole State, as it is the only port and the only place from whence the people can procure those Articles of foreign produce which are essential to their support, and it in great measure serves to cover and keep in subjection the State of Georgia. From thence, the enemy can also establish small posts in North Carolina. And if they maintain a post in Chesapeak, they keep up the appearance of possessing 400 Miles upon the Coast and of consequence have a pretext for setting up claims which may be very detrimental to the interests of America in European Councils.

We are not sufficiently acquainted with the position of Charles town, neither it is necessary at this time, to enter into a detail of the proper mode of attacking it, or of the probability which we should have of succeeding. For these we will refer your Excellency to Brigadier Genl. du portail Commander of the Corps of Engineers in the service of the United States, who will have the honor of presenting this. That Gentleman having been in Charles town as principal Engineer during the greater part of the seige, and in the Environs of it as a prisoner of War a considerable time afterwards, had opportunities of making very full observations, which he judiciously improved.

A variety of cases different from those we have stated may occur. It is for this reason that we have thought proper to send General du portail to your Excellency. He is fully acquainted with every circumstance of our Affairs in this quarter, and we recommend him to your Excellency as an Officer upon whose Abilities and in whose integrity you may place the fullest confidence.

We would observe to your Excellency that it will be very essential to the dispatch of the business in contemplation for you to send up to Elk River at the Head of Chesapeak Bay all your Frigates, Transports and Vessels proper for the conveyance of the French and American Troops down the Bay. We shall endeavour to have as many as can be found in Baltimore and other ports secured, but we have reason to believe they will be very few. We have the honor etc.

Document 5-f†

Entries from Washington's Diaries, August, 1781

[August] 19*th.* The want of Horses, or bad condition of them in the French Army delayed the March till this day; the same causes, it is to be feared, will occasion a slow and disagreeable March to Elk if fresh horses cannot be procured and better management of them adopted.

The detachment from the American [Army] is composed of the light Infantry under Scammell, two light companies of York to be joined by the like Number from the Connecticut line, the Remainder of the Jersey line, two Regiments of York, Hazens Regiment and the Regiment of Rhode Island, together with Lambs Regiment of Artillery with Cannon and other Ordnance for the field and Siege.

Hazens Regiment being thrown over at Dobbs' ferry was ordered with the Jersey Troops to March and take Post on the heights between Springfield and Chatham and cover a french Bakery at the latter place to veil our real movements and create apprehensions for Staten Island.

The Quarter Master Genl. was dispatched to Kings ferry, the only secure passage, to prepare for the speedy transportation of the Troops across the River.

Passed Sing sing with the American column. The French column Marched by the way of Northcastle, Crompond, and Pinesbridge, being near ten miles further.

†From: John Fitzpatrick, ed., *George Washington's Diaries* (Boston: Houghton Mifflin Co., 1925), vol. 2, pp. 255-56.

20*th*. The head of the Americans arrived at Kings ferry about ten o'clock and immediately began to cross.

21*st*. In the course of this day the whole of the American Troops, all their baggage, artillery and Stores, crossed the River; nothing remained of ours but some Waggons in the Commissarys. and Qr. Mr. Generals departmt. which were delayed, that no interruption might be given to the passage of the French Army.

During the passing of the French Army I mounted 30 flat Boats (able to carry about 40 Men each) upon carriages, as well with a design to deceive the enemy as to our real movement, as to be useful to me in Virginia when I get there.

Some of the french Artillery wch. preceeded their Infantry got to the ferry and crossed it also.

6

The British Assess the Situation: Clinton to Cornwallis, August, 1781

Document†

Clinton to Cornwallis
New-York, August 27th, 1781.

My Lord, I had the honour to receive your Lordship's letter in cypher of the 17th instant, by the Swallow dispatch boat, which arrived here the 23d. In answer to which, I must confess that I conceived your letter of the 27th ultimo, gave me reason to suppose it was your intention to send me the troops you could spare; as soon as you finished the evacuation of Portsmouth; and I was impatient for their arrival for the reasons I have already communicated to you, as it is probable they would have been of infinite use had they come in time. For on the arrival of the two thousand five hundred raw German recruits which I mentioned in my last, and in the hope of reinforcement from your Lordship, I had assembled my little army in such a manner as to be able to avail myself of any opportunity which might be given me by the enemy, who had foraged within six miles of my lines on the 17th. This small movement was made on the 18th, they fell back on the 19th, and passed the Croton; afterwards crossed the Hudson at King's ferry, and are now encamped in the neighbourhood of Chatham.

I cannot well ascertain Mr. Washington's real intentions by this move of his army; but it is possible he means for the present to suspend his offensive operations against this post, and to take a defensive station at the old post of Morris-town, from whence he may detach to the southward. On this account therefore, and because the season is approaching when operation may recommence in the Chesapeak, I request your Lordship will be pleased to keep with you all the troops you have there, and I shall send you such recruits, convalescents, &c. as can go by this sudden opportunity; which are all that I can at present spare; as this move of the enemy may be only a feint, and they may return to their former position, which they certainly will do, if De Grasse arrives. But towards the latter end of next month, when the effects

†From: B.F. Stevens, ed., *The Clinton-Cornwallis Controversy*, vol. 2, pp. 141-43.

of the equinox are over, (for I am persuaded the Admiral will not approve of any water movements till then) if this post should not be threatened, I propose to reinforce the Chesapeak army with all the troops which can possibly be spared consistently with the security of this important post.

General Leslie has been here some days, he will himself explain to your Lordship the cause of his coming. I was much concerned to find him in so bad a state of health on his arrival, but it is now much altered for the better; he embarks to-morrow to proceed to Chesapeak on his way to Charlestown.

If your Lordship from your knowledge of the state of South-Carolina, should be opinion that any troops may be spared from thence, I beg leave to suggest that the sooner you give orders for their joining you the better.

I have the honour to be, &c.

H. CLINTON.

7

Washington and Lafayette Prepare for Battle: Washington to Lafayette, September, 1781

Document†

Washington to Lafayette

Head Quarters, Philadelphia, September 2, 1781.
Nothing, My dear Marquis could have afforded me greater satisfaction than the information communicated in your two Letters of the 21st. and 24th. Ulto of the measures you had taken and the Arrangements you were making, in consequence of the Intelligence I had given you.

Calculating upon the regular force under your immediate Orders, the Militia which have already been called for and may be expected in the field; the whole of the French Army, and the American Corps now marching with Major Gen. Lincoln from the Northward in addition to the land Forces expected on board the Fleet; I flatter myself we shall not experience any considerable difficulties from the want of Men to carry our most favourite Projects into execution. The means for prosecuting a Seige with rapidity, energy, and success, and of supplying the Troops while they are engaged in that service (as they are more precarious) have been and still continue to be the great objects of my concern and attention.

Heavy Cannon, Ordnance Stores and Ammunition to a pretty large Amount, are now forwarding. General Knox, in whose immediate province these Arrangements are, who knows our whole resources, is making every exertion to furnish a competent supply, and will be on the spot to remedy every deficiency, as far as the circumstances will possibly admit.

Having also, from the first moment, been extremely anxious respecting the *Supplies* of the Army (in which, I comprehended not only Provisions of the Bread and Meat kind &c but also Forage and the means of transportation) I had written pressingly to the Governors of Maryland and Virginia on that

†From: Fitzpatrick, ed., *Writings of George Washington*, vol. 23, pp. 75-77.

subject previous to the receipt of your favor of the 21st of August. I have since reiterated my Entreaties, and enforced in the strongest terms I was capable of using, the Requisitions for Specific Supplies made by Congress, and now again called for by the Superintendt of Finance from the States of Jersey, Delaware, and Maryland, and as to the supplies of Pennsylvania, we are to look for them, from the Financier himself. I hope and trust the efforts of these States and of Virginia will be uncommonly great and proportionate to the Magnitude of the object before us.

In Order to introduce some kind of System and Method in our Supplies, to know with certainty what may be depended upon, and to put the business in the best possible train of execution, I shall send forward the Heads of Departments as soon as their presence can be dispensed with. I have spoken to the Surgeon General respecting Hospital Stores and Medicines, all that can be done will be done in that department.

As to Cloathing I am sorry to inform you, little is to be expected, except in the Article of Shoes, of which a full supply will be sent on.

In my progress to the Southward, I shall take care, as far as practicable, to make all the Arrangements necessary for the Operation in view, and to impress the Executives, with an idea of the absolute necessity of furnishing their quotas of Supplies regularly, as we have no other resources to rely upon for the support of the Army, and especially, as I am very apprehensive, that a quantity of 1500 Barrels of salted Provisions which I had ordered to be shipped under Convoy of the Count de Barras, did not arrive in time for that purpose.

But my dear Marquis, I am distressed beyond expression, to know what is become of the Count de Grasse, and for fear the English Fleet, by occupying the Chesapeake (towards which my last accounts say they were steering) should frustrate all our flattering prospects in that quarter. I am also not a little solicitous for the Count de Barras, who was to have sailed from Rhode Island on the 23d Ulto. and from whom I have heard nothing since that time. Of many contingencies we will hope for the most propitious events.

Should the retreat of Lord Cornwallis by water, be cut off by the arrival of either of the French Fleets, I am persuaded you will do all in your power to prevent his escape by land. May that great felicity be reserved for you!

You See, how critically important the present Moment is: for my own part I am determined still to persist, with unremitting ardour in my present Plan, unless some inevitable and insuperable obstacles are thrown in our way.

Adieu my Dear Marquis! If you get any thing New from any quarter, send it I pray you *on the Spur of Speed*, for I am almost all impatience and anxiety, at the same time, that I am etc.

8

Hood's "Sentiments Upon the Truly Unfortunate Day": Graves and de Grasse Meet at Sea

Document†

Notes by Rear Admiral Hood

Coast of Virginia, 6th of September, 1781.

Yesterday the British fleet had a rich and most plentiful harvest of glory in view, but the means to gather it were omitted in more instances than one.

I may begin with observing that the enemy's van was not very closely attacked as it came out of Lynn Haven Bay, which, I think, might have been done with clear advantage, as they came out by no means in a regular and connected way. When the enemy's van was out it was greatly extended beyond the centre and rear, and might *have* been attacked with the whole force of the British fleet. Had such an attack been made, several of the enemy's ships must have been inevitably demolished in half an hour's action, and there was a full hour and half to have engaged it before any of the rear could have come up.

Thirdly, when the van of the two fleets got into action, and the ships of the British line were hard pressed, one (the Shrewsbury) totally disabled very early from keeping her station by having her fore and main topsail yards shot away, which left her second (the Intrepid) exposed to two ships of superior force, which the noble and spirited behaviour of Captain Molloy obliged to turn their sterns to him, that the signal was not thrown out for the van ships to make more sail to have enabled the centre to push on to the support of the

†From: French E. Chadwick, ed., *The Graves Papers* (New York: Naval History Society, 1916), pp. 89-91.

van, instead of engaging at such an improper distance (the London having her main topsail to the mast the whole time she was firing with the signal for the line at half a cable flying), that the second ship astern of the London received but trifling damage, and the third astern of her (the London) received no damage at all, which most clearly proves how much too great the distance was the centre division engaged.

Now, had the centre gone to the support of the van, and the signal for the line been hauled down, or the commander-in-chief had set the example of close action, even with the signal for the line flying, the van of the enemy must have been cut to pieces, and the rear division of the British fleet would have been opposed to those ships the centre division fired at, and at the proper distance for engaging, or the Rear-Admiral who commanded it would have a great deal to answer for. Instead of that, our centre division did the enemy but little damage, and our rear ships being barely within random shot, three only fired a few shot. So soon as the signal for the line was hauled down at twenty-five minutes after five the rear division bore up, above half a mile to leeward of the centre division, but the French ships bearing up also, it did not near them, and at twenty-five minutes after six the signal of the line ahead at half a cable being again hoisted, and the signal for battle hauled down, Rear-Admiral Sir S. Hood called to the Monarch (his leader) to keep her wind, as he dared not separate his division just at dark, the London not bearing up at all.

N.B.—This forenoon Captain Everett came on board the Barfleur with a message from Rear-Admiral Graves to Rear-Admiral Sir S. Hood, desiring his opinion whether the action should be renewed. Sir Samuel's answer was: 'I dare say Mr. Graves will do what is right; I can *send* no opinion, but whenever he, Mr. Graves, wishes to see me, I will wait upon him with great pleasure.'

9

The Strategy of the Allies: Formation for Attack on Yorktown

Document 9-a†

De Grasse to Washington, September, 1781

Cape Henry, Sept. 2, 1781.

Sir: I received at the moment when I least expected it the letter which Your Excellency has had the kindness to transmit to me through M. du Portail, whose reputation has been known to me for many years. Therefore, I have not hesitated to open my heart to him and to acquaint him with all my resources and my orders. I am as concerned as it is possible to be that I have not with me any other ships than my men-of-war, which are too large to be used for the transport of American and French troops from the river Elk to Chesapeake Bay, and four frigates only, which take the place of very small vessels, and are at this moment, employed to guard the James river, in order to prevent the retreat of Lord Cornwallis on the Carolina side. I have also a few ships blockading the mouth of the York river, and I am with the rest of my army at Cape Henry ready to engage the enemy's maritime forces, should they come to the relief of Lord Cornwallis, whom I regard as blockaded until the arrival of Your Excellency and of your army. The union of my three thousand men with the forces of the Marquis de la Fayette ought to take place at James-town the 5th of this month. My men are on the rivers in launches and canoes of the army and I expect their arrival tomorrow in the course of the day.

Lord Cornwallis is at present at York where he is fortifying himself by land and sea. He is also holding the post of Gloucester on the other side of the river, and he has fortified the neck of the peninsula. He has the *Charon* of 44 cannons and several sloops of war with the frigate, the *Gaudeloupe*, which ran to shelter the day of my arrival pursued by men-of-war and frigates, which seized the *Loyalist*, a sloop of 22 cannons. I have in the river James,

†From: Institut Francais de Washington, *Correspondence of General Washington and Comte de Grasse* (Washington, D.C.: Government Printing Office, 1931), pp. 8-11.

the *Experiment,* of 44 cannons, the *Andromaque,* a frigate of 30 and three sloops of from 16 to 20 cannons, which I luckily seized the day previous to landing in this Bay. Your Excellency will perceive that with so few ships suitable for the different rivers that must be entered in order to attack the strong places of these regions, I am very poorly equipped for assisting in your plans. Happily, we have drawn up at the spot where I can be of use, but with no means for hastening the arrival of Your Excellency, and I am told it is impossible to find any in this immense river. I fear that the time at my disposal will not permit me to give all the aid to the united forces which I should wish to procure them. I had resolved to attack York with the Marquis de la Fayette's troops and those which I brought in my ships. But because of the letter which I received from Your Excellency, and on the advice of M. du Portail, I have suspended my plans until the arrival of the Generals, whose experience in the profession of arms, knowledge of the country and insight will greatly augment our resources. I am persuaded that my army, who are inflamed only with the desire to give proof of their courage, will surpass themselves under the eyes of Generals worthy to appreciate them. Until that moment I shall devote my entire attention to the means of facilitating all the attacks you will judge proper to make on your arrival against the army of Lord Cornwallis. This is the only practical plan, since he is giving us the opportunity by the position he has taken in altogether abandoning Portsmouth on the river James.

I could give, in case of need, eighteen hundred men of good troops chosen from the garrisons of the fleet, and I could furnish land and siege cannons. These, it is true, could only be fired from naval gun rests, but their bullets create quite as much disturbance as if they were mounted on gun carriages used on land, and for sieges. The arrival of the squadron of M. du Barras, to whom I have written to come to join me, should be useful to us, according to what M. du Portail says, because of the stores with which it is furnished.

I have the honor to be with a respectful attachment,
Your Excellency's
Most humble and most obedient servant,

Comte de Grasse.

Document 9-b†

Washington to de Grasse, September, 1781
QUESTIONS PROPOSED BY
GENERAL WASHINGTON TO COMTE DE GRASSE
September 17, 1781.

The noble and generous Support which is given to this Country, by His Most Christian Majesty, does, as it ought, fill the breast of every American with gratitude and Love; The zeal and alacrity with which His Officers strive

†From: Fitzpatrick, ed., *Writings of George Washington,* vol. 23, pp. 122-25.

to carry his Royal intentions into execution, merit our highest admiration and applause; a recent instance of this is now before us; But the distressed and unfortunate circumstances of these United States, and the dispersed situation of their Troops are such, as do not admit their Military operations to be carried on with that celerity which could be wished, nor place them in that advantageous ground, from which they may reap all that benefit from this generous Aid, that in other circumstances they might expect to receive.

The measures which are now pursuing, are big with great events; the Peace and Independence of this Country, and the general tranquility of Europe will, it is more than probable, result from our Compleat success; disgrace to ourselves, Triumph to the Enemy; and probable Ruin to the American Cause, will follow our disappointment. The first is certain, if the powerfull Fleet, now in Chesapeak Bay or such part of it as will be competent to the purpose, can remain to the close of a regular Operation, which, from various unforeseen causes, may be protracted beyond our present expectation. The second is much to be apprehended, if from the fear of loosing the Aid of the Fleet, the operations by Land are precipitated faster than a necessary prudence and regard to the lives of Men, will warrant; the first may be slow, but sure; the second must be bloody and precarious.

Under this state of matters, General Washington begs, that the Count de Grasse will have the goodness to give him a Resolution of the following Questions. Viz.

QUESTIONS

1st. Is your Excellency restricted to any certain time for the continuance of the Fleet upon this Coast? If any time is fixed, beyond which your Orders will not warrant your stay in this Bay, or if the pursuit of any other object should more attract your attention, be pleased to name the day to which your departure is determined.

2d. If your Excellency should find yourself under a necessity to return the Troops, under the Command of the Marquis de St. Simon, to the West Indies, (however to be lamented such circumstance must be) may I not be assured, that a detachment of the Fleet may be imployed as a Convoy to those Troops, and that the Main Fleet may remain in the Bay to form a sufficient cover to our Operations against the Enemy, to prevent their receiving supplies by water, and to protect us from any attempt from the British to give relief to Lord Cornwallis and raise our Seige; and this Fleet to remain untill the close of our Operations.

3d. Will it, in your Excellency's opinion, be practicable to force with your Ships, the passage of the York River, so as to git above the Enemy?

This measure, if effected, will be attended with almost infinite advantages, not only, as it will secure our Communication on both sides the River, which otherwise must be very lengthy and tedious, but will give us the Navigation of the River, and enable us to draw the supplies of the Country throughout its whole extent; and will also form the compleat investiture of the Enemy's Posts.

4th. So long as the Enemy possesses both sides of the River, it will be necessary to keep up our force on both sides, to aid our efforts in the operation, will it be in your Excellency's power to spare us any number of Men from on board the Fleet, to continue so long as this measure is necessary? if any, what number?

5th. If in the prosecution of our operations, our prospects of success shuld wear a favorable Aspect, I shall be glad to be decided, whether your Excellency will be able to detach some suitable Vessels from your Fleet, sufficient to block in the British Troops at Wilmington, and to possess the Harbour of Charlestown?

6th. If our Operations should be of such a nature as to require it, will your Excellency be able to lend us some heavy Cannon and other Artillery, [Powder also, in what number and quantity?

Document 9-c†

Washington to de Grasse, September, 1781

Williamsburg, September 25, 1781.

Sir: I cannot conceal from your Excellency the painful anxiety under which I have laboured since the receipt of the letter with which you honored me on the 23d inst.

The naval movements which Your Excellency states there as possible considering the intelligence communicated to you by the baron de Clossen, make it incumbent upon me to represent the consequences that wd arise from them, and to urge a perseverance in the plan already agreed upon. Give me leave in the first place to repeat to Yr Excellency that the enterprise against York under the protection of your Ships, is as certain as any military operation can be rendered by a decisive superiority of strength and means; that it is in fact reducible to calculation, and that the surrender of the british Garrison will be so important in itself and its consequences, that it must necessarily go a great way towards terminating the war, and securing the invaluable objects of it to the Allies.

Your Excellency's departure from the Chesapeake by affordg an opening for the succour of York, which the enemy wd instantly avail himself of, would frustrate these brilliant prospects, and the consequence would be not only the disgrace and loss of renouncing an enterprise, upon which the fairest expectations of the Allies have been founded, after the most expensive preparations and uncommon exertions and fatigues; but the disbanding perhaps the whole Army for want of provisions.

The present Theatre of the War is totally deficient in means of land transportation, being intersected by large rivers, and the whole dependance for interior communication being upon small Vessels. The Country has been much exhausted besides by the ravages of the enemy and the subsistence of our own Army; that our supplies can only be drawn from a distance and under cover of a fleet Mistress of the Chesapeake.

†From: Ibid., pp. 136-39.

I most earnestly entreat Your Excellency farther to consider that if the present opportunity shd be missed; that if you shld withdraw your maritime force from the position agreed upon, that no future day can restore us a similar occasion for striking a decisive blow; that the british will be indefatigable in strengthening their most important maritime points, and that the epoch of an honorable peace will be more remote than ever.

The confidence with which I feel myself inspired by the energy of character and the naval talents which so eminently distinguish Yr Excellency leaves me no doubt that upon a consideration of the consequences which must follow your departure from the Chesapeake, that Yr Excellency will determine upon the possible measure which the dearest interests of the common cause wd dictate.

I had invariably flattered myself from the accounts given me by skilful mariners, that Your Excellys position, moored in the Chesapeake might be made so respectable, as to bid defiance to any attempt on the pt of the british fleet, at the same time that it wd support the operations of a seige, secure the transportation of our supplies by water and oeconomise the most precious time by facilitating the debarkation of our heavy Artillery and stores conveniently to the trenches in York River. It is to be observed that the strength of the enemy's reinforcement announced under Admiral Digby as we have the intelligence from the british, may not only be exaggerated, but altogether a finesse, and supposing the account consistent with truth: their total force it was hoped wd. not put them in condition to attack with any prospect of success.

If the stationary position which had been agreed upon should be found utterly impracticable, there is an alternative which however inferior considered relatively to the support and facility of our land operations would save our affairs from ruin; this is to cruise with Your Excellency's fleet within view of the capes, so as effectually to prevent the entrance of any british Vessels.

Upon the whole, I shd. esteem myself deficient in my duty to the common cause of France and America, if I did not persevere in entreating Yr. Excellency to resume the plans that have been so happily arranged, and if invincible maritime reasons prevent, I depend as a last resource upon Your Excellency's pursuing the alternative above mentioned and rendering the Chesapeake inaccessible to any Enemys Vessel.

However the british Admiral may manoeuvre and endeavour to divert Yr Excellency from the object in view, I can hardly admit a belief that it can be his serious intention to engage in a general action with a Fleet whose force will be superior supposing the most flattering accounts for the british to be true; past experience having taught them to engage with caution even upon equal terms, and forced from them acknowledgements, which prove the respect with which they have been inspired.

Let me add Sir that even a momentary absence of the french fleet may expose us to the loss of the british Garrison at York as in the present state of affairs Ld Cornwallis might effect the evacuation with the loss of his Artillery and baggage and such a sacrifice of men as his object would evidently justify.

The Marquis de la fayette who does me the honor to bear this to Yr Excellency will explain many peculiarities of our situation which could not well be comprised in a letter; his candour and abilities are well known to Yr Excellency and entitle him to the fullest confidence in treating the most important interests. I have earnestly requested him not to proceed any farther than the Capes for fear of accidents shd Yr. Excellency have put to sea; in this case he will dispatch a Letter to Yr Excellency in addition to this. I have the honor etc.

Document 9-d†

Washington's General Orders, September, 1781

Head Quarters, Williamsburgh,
Thursday, September 27, 1781
Parole Virginia. Countersigns York, Gloscester.

Officers of the day for Tomorrow
{ Major General Lincoln.
Colonel Dayton.
Lt. Col. Antill.
B.M. Hobbey.

The Rolls are to be called with the greatest strictness at retreat beating this evening and again at tattoo in presence of the Field Officers, at which time no Officer or soldier in condition to March is to be absent from his Post in Camp. The General confides in the Commanders of Corps for the punctual execution of these orders.

Till circumstances shall render a change of disposition Necessary, the following will be the order of Battle for the Army, the American Troops composing the right Wing will be formed into two Lines, the Continental Forces in the front line, consisting of the following devisions and in the following order viz. Muhlenberghs and Hazens Brigades to form The Division on the right under the Command of the Marquis de la Fayette, Waynes and the Maryland Brigade, the Division of the centre for the present to be commanded by Baron de Stueben, Daytons and Clintons Brigades, that on the Left. The senior Continental Officer will Command the Right Wing and his Excellency Count Rochambeau the Left Wing of which he will be pleased to make his own disposition.

The two Companies of Delaware are for the present to be annexed to the 3d Maryland Regiment.

Stephens and Lawson Brigades of Militia will form the second Line, the Park of Artillery, the Corps of Sappers and Miners and the Virginia State Regiment will be posted between the two Lines in the order above Mentioned, commencing from the right.

The whole Army will March by the right in one Column at 5 oClock tomorrow Morning precisely. The particular order of March for the right Wing will be distributed by the Quarter Master General.

†From: Ibid., pp. 146-48.

The General desires that the Officers will confine themselves in point of Baggage to objects of the first Necessity, that the Army may March as light and unincumbered as possible. The Quarter Master General will have directions to appoint a proper deposit for the effects that will be left, from whence they will be transported to the Army as soon as a parmenent position is taken.

The Quarter Master General will allot a proportionate Number of the Waggons in his possession for the service of the Left Wing.

If the Enemy should be tempted to Meet the Army on its March, the General particularly enjoins the troops to place their principle relyance on the Bayonet, that they may prove the Vanity of the Boast which the British make of their particular prowess in deciding Battles with that Weapon. He trusts that a generous Emulation will actuate the Allied Armies, that the french whose National Weapon is that of close fight, and the troops in General that have so often used it with success will distinguish themselves on every Occasion that offers; the Justice of the cause in which we are engaged and the *Honor* of the two Nations must inspire every breast with sentiments that are the presage of Victory.

General Muhlenberghs Brigade of Infantry with the Artillery attached to it, preceded by Colonel Lewises Corps of Rifle men and the light Dragoons will form the advanced Guard. The present Camp Guards the rear guard under the Command of Major Ried. It will form on the great Road on the left and in the rear of the encampment at five oClock.

10

The British Defeat

Document 10-a†

Clinton to Cornwallis, September, 1781

Sir Henry Clinton, K.B. to Earl Cornwallis, dated
New York, Sept. 24, 1781. [In Cypher.]
[Received September 29, 1781.]

My Lord, I was honoured yesterday with your Lordship's letter of the 16th and 17th instant, and at a meeting of the General and Flag Officers held this day, it is determined, that above five thousand men, rank and file, shall be embarked on board the King's ships, and the joint exertions of the navy and army made in a few days to relieve you, and afterwards co-operate with you.

The fleet consists of twenty-three sail of the line, three of which are three deckers. There is every reason to hope we start from hence the 5th October. I have received your Lordship's letter of the 8th instant.

I have the honour to be, &c. H. Clinton.

P.S. Admiral Digby is this moment arrived at the Hook, with three sail of the line.

At a venture, without knowing whether they can be seen by us, I request, that if all is well, upon hearing a considerable firing towards the entrance of the Chesapeake, three large separate smokes may be made parallel to it; and, if you possess the post of Gloucester, four.

I shall send another runner soon. H. Clinton.

Document 10-b‡

Clinton to Cornwallis, September, 1781

September 30, 1781. [Duplicate, in Cypher.]

My Lord, Your Lordship may be assured that I am doing every thing in my power to relieve you by a direct move, and I have reason to hope, from the assurances given me this day by Admiral Graves, that we may pass the bar by the 12th of October, if the winds permit, and no unforeseen accident happens: this, however, is subject to disappointment, wherefore, if I hear from you, your wishes will of course direct me, and I shall persist in my idea of a direct move, even to the middle of November, should it be your

---

†From B.F. Stevens, ed., *Clinton-Cornwallis Controversy*, Vol. 2, pp. 159-60.
‡From: Ibid., vol. 2, pp. 172-73.

Lordship's opinion that you can hold out so long; but if, when I hear from you, you tell me that you cannot, and I am without hopes of arriving in time to succour you by a direct move, I will immediately make an attempt upon Philadelphia by land, giving you notice, if possible, of my intention. If this should draw any part of Washington's force from you, it may possibly give you an opportunity of doing something to save your army; of which, however, you can best judge from being upon the spot.

I have the honour to be, &c. H. Clinton.

Document 10-c†

Cornwallis to Clinton, October, 1781

York-Town, October 15, 1781. [In Cypher.]

Sir, Last evening the enemy carried my two advanced redoubts on the left by storm, and during the night have included them in their second parallel, which they are at present busy in perfecting. My situation now becomes very critical; we dare not shew a gun to their old batteries, and I expect that their new ones will open to-morrow morning; experience has shewn that our fresh earthen works do not resist their powerful artillery, so that we shall soon be exposed to an assault in ruined works, in a bad position, and with weakened numbers. The safety of the place is, therefore, so precarious, that I cannot recommend that the fleet and army should run great risque in endeavouring to save us.

I have the honour to be, &c. Cornwallis.

†From: Ibid., p. 188.

11

Cornwallis Surrenders: Cornwallis to Clinton, October,1781

Document†

Cornwallis to Clinton
York Town, Virginia, October 20, 1781.

Sir, I have the mortification to inform your Excellency that I have been forced to give up the posts of York and Gloucester, and to surrender the troops under my command, by capitulation on the 19th inst. as prisoners of war to the combined forces of America and France.

I never saw this post in a very favourable light, but when I found·I was to be attacked in it in so unprepared a state, by so powerful an army and artillery, nothing but the hopes of relief would have induced me to attempt its defence; for I would either have endeavoured to escape to New-York, by rapid marches from the Gloucester side, immediately on the arrival of General Washington's troops at Williamsburgh, or I would notwithstanding the disparity of numbers have attacked them in the open field, where it might have been just possible that fortune would have favoured the gallantry of the handful of troops under my command: but being assured by your Excellency's letters, that every possible means would be tried by the navy and army to relieve us, I could not think myself at liberty to venture upon either of those desperate attempts; therefore, after remaining for two days in a strong position in front of this place, in hopes of being attacked, upon observing that the enemy were taking measures, which could not fail of turning my left flank in a short time, and receiving on the second evening your letter of the 24th of September, informing that the relief would sail about the 5th of October, I withdrew within the works on the night of the 29th of September, hoping by the labour and firmness of the soldiers, to protract the defence until you could arrive. Every thing was to be expected from the spirit of the troops, but every disadvantage attended their labour, as the works were to be continued under the enemy's fire, and our stock of intrenching tools, which did not much exceed four hundred, when we began to work in the latter end of August, was now much diminished.

The enemy broke ground on the night of the 30th, and constructed on

†From: Ibid., pp. 205-16.

that night, and the two following days and nights, two redoubts, which, with some works that had belonged to our outward position, occupied a gorge between two creeks or ravines, which come from the river on each side of the town. On the night of the 6th of October they made their first parallel, extending from its right on the river to a deep ravine on the left, nearly opposite to the center of this place, and embracing our whole left at the distance of six hundred yards. Having perfected this parallel, their batteries opened on the evening of the 9th, against our left, and other batteries fired at the same time against a redoubt, advanced over the Creek upon our right, and defended by about one hundred and twenty men of the 23d regiment and marines, who maintained that post with uncommon gallantry. The fire continued incessant from heavy cannon and from mortars and howitzes, throwing shells from eight to sixteen inches, until all our guns on the left were silenced, our work much damaged, and our loss of men considerable. On the night of the 11th they began their second parallel, about three hundred yards nearer to us; the troops being much weakened by sickness as well as by the fire of the besiegers, and observing that the enemy had not only secured their flanks, but proceeded in every respect with the utmost regularity and caution, I could not venture so large sorties, as to hope from them any considerable effect; but otherwise, I did every thing in my power to interrupt this work, by opening new embrazures for guns, and keeping up a constant fire with all the howitzes and small mortars that we could man. On the evening of the 14th, they assaulted and carried two redoubts that had been advanced about three hundred yards for the purpose of delaying their approaches, and covering our left flank, and during the night included them in their second parallel, on which they continued to work with the utmost exertion. Being perfectly sensible that our works could not stand many hours after the opening of the batteries of that parallel, we not only continued a constant fire with all our mortars, and every gun that could be brought to bear upon it, but a little before day break on the morning of the 16th, I ordered a sortie of about three hundred and fifty men under the direction of Lieutenant-colonel Abercrombie to attack two batteries, which appeared to be in the greatest forwardness, and to spike the guns. A detachment of guards with the eightieth company of Grenadiers, under the command of Lieutenant-colonel Lake attacked the one, and one of Light Infantry under the command of Major Armstrong attacked the other, and both succeeded by forcing the redoubts that covered them, spiking eleven guns, and killing or wounding about one hundred of the French troops, who had the guard of that part of the trenches, and with little loss on our side. This action, though extremely honourable to the officers and soldiers who executed it, proved of little public advantage, for the cannon having been spiked in a hurry, were soon rendered fit for service again, and before dark the whole parallel and batteries appeared to be nearly complete. At this time we knew that there was no part of the whole front attacked, on which we could show a single gun, and our shells were nearly expended; I therefore had only to chuse between preparing to surrender next day, or endeavouring to get off with the greatest part of the troops, and I determined to attempt the latter, reflecting that though it should prove unsuccessful in its immediate object, it might at least delay the enemy in the prosecution of further enterprizes: sixteen large boats were prepared, and upon other pretexts were ordered to be in readiness to receive troops precisely at ten o'clock. With these I hoped to pass the infantry during the night, abandoning our baggage, and leaving a detachment to capitulate for the town's people, and the sick and wounded; on which subject a letter was ready to be delivered to General Washington. After making my arrangements with the utmost secrecy, the Light Infantry, greatest part of the Guards, and part of the twenty-third regiment landed at Gloucester; but at this critical moment, the weather from being moderate and calm, changed to a most violent storm of wind and rain, and drove all the boats, some of which had troops on board, down the river. It was soon evident that the intended passage was impracticable, and the absence of the boats rendered it equally impossible to bring back the troops that had passed; which I had ordered about two in the morning. In this situation, with my little force divided, the enemy's batteries opened at day break; the passage between this place and Gloucester was much exposed, but the boats having now returned, they were ordered to bring back the troops that had passed during the night, and they joined us in the forenoon without much loss. Our works in the mean time were going to ruin, and not having been able to strengthen them by abbatis, nor in any other manner but by a slight fraizing which the enemy's artillery were demolishing wherever they fired, my opinion entirely coincided with that of the engineer and principal officers of the army, that they were in many places assailable in the forenoon, and that by the continuence of the same fire for a few hours longer, they would be in such a state as to render it desperate with our numbers to attempt to maintain them. We at that time could not fire a single gun, only one eight-inch and little more than an hundred cohorn shells remained; a diversion by the French ships of war that lay at the mouth of York-river, was to be expected. Our numbers had been diminished by the enemy's fire, but particularly by sickness, and the strength and spirits of those in the works were much exhausted by the fatigue of constant watching and unremitting duty. Under all these circumstances, I thought it would have been wanton and inhuman to the last degree to sacrifice the lives of this small body of gallant soldiers, who had ever behaved with so much fidelity and courage, by exposing them to an assault, which from the numbers and precautions of the enemy could not fail to succeed. I therefore proposed to capitulate, and I have the honour to inclose to your Excellency the copy of the correspondence between General Washington and me on that subject, and the terms of capitulation agreed upon. I sincerely lament that better could not be obtained, but I have neglected nothing in my power to alleviate the misfortune and distress of both officers and soldiers. The men are well cloathed and provided with necessaries, and I trust will be regularly supplied by the means of the officers that are permitted to remain with them. The treatment, in general, that we have received from the enemy since our surrender, has been perfectly good and proper; but the kindness and attention that has been shewn to us by the French officers in particular, their delicate sensibility of our situation, their generous and pressing offer of money both public and private, to any amount, has really gone beyond what I can possibly describe, and will, I hope, make an impression on the breast of every British officer, whenever the fortune of war should put any of them into our power.

Although the event has been so unfortunate, the patience of the soldiers in bearing the greatest fatigues, and their firmness and intrepidity under a persevering fire of shot and shells, that I believe has not often been exceeded, deserved the highest admiration and praise. A successful defence, however, in our situation was perhaps impossible, for the place could only be reckoned an intrenched camp, subject in most places to enfilade, and the ground in general so disadvantageous, that nothing but the necessity of fortifying it as a post to protect the navy, could have induced any person to erect works upon it. Our force diminished daily by sickness and other losses, and was reduced when we offered to capitulate on this side to little more than three thousand two hundred rank and file fit for duty, including officers, servants, and artificers; and at Gloucester about six hundred, including cavalry. The enemy's army consisted of upwards of eight thousand French, nearly as many continentals, and five thousand militia. They brought an immense train of heavy artillery, most amply furnished with ammunition, and perfectly well manned.

The constant and universal chearfulness and spirit of the officers in all hardships and danger, deserve my warmest acknowledgments; and I have been particularly indebted to Brigadier-general O'Hara, and to Lieutenant-colonel Abercrombie, the former commanding on the right and the latter on the left, for their attention and exertion on every occasion. The detachment of the twenty-third regiment of Marines in the redoubt on the right, commanded by Captain Apthorpe, and the subsequent detachments commanded by Lieutenant-colonel Johnson, deserve particular commendation. Captain Rochfort who commanded the artillery, and indeed every officer and soldier of that distinguished corps; and Lieutenant Sutherland the commanding Engineer have merited in every respect my highest approbation; and I cannot sufficiently acknowledge my obligations to Captain Symonds, who commanded his Majesty's ships, and to the other officers and seamen of the navy for their active and zealous co-operation.

I transmit returns of our killed and wounded the loss of seamen and townspeople was likewise considerable.

I trust that your Excellency will please to hasten the return of the Bonetta, after landing her passengers, in compliance with the article of capitulation.

Lieutenant-colonel Abercrombie will have the honour to deliver this dispatch, and is well qualified to explain to your Excellency every particular relating to our past and present situation.

I have the honour to be, &c. Cornwallis.

Part three

Bibliographic Essay

The most valuable sources for a study of the events leading to Cornwallis's surrender at Yorktown are the letters of the commanding officers. Washington's voluminous correspondence is found in John C. Fitzpatrick, ed., *The Writings of George Washington*, 39 vols. (Washington D.C., 1931-1944), of which volumes 19-23 pertain to the period 1780-1781. Fitzpatrick is also the editor of *George Washington's Diaries*, 4 vols. (Boston, 1925), with volume 2 covering the period 1780-1781.

Letters to Washington are found in Jared Sparks, ed., *The Correspondence of the American Revolution; Being Letters of Eminent Men to George Washington*, 4 vols. (Boston, 1853). Also see S. Hamilton, ed., *Letters to Washington and Accompanying Papers*, 5 vols. (Boston, 1898-1902). Letters between Washington and Admiral de Grasse are found in *Correspondence of General Washington and Comte de Grasse*, edited by the Institut Français de Washington (Washington, D.C., 1931).

The correspondence of Lord Cornwallis, Sir Henry Clinton, and other British officers as well as Lord George Germain is found in B.F. Stevens, ed., *The Campaign in Virginia, 1781; An Exact Reprint of Six Rare Pamphlets in the Clinton-Cornwallis Controversy*, 2 vols. (London, 1888). Letters of Cornwallis can also be found in *Correspondence of Charles, first Marquis Cornwallis*, 3 vols. (London, 1859). *The Graves Papers*, French E. Chadwick, ed. (New York, 1916), contains correspondence relating to the Battle of the Capes and other naval events. Also see David Hanny, ed., *Letters Written by Sir Samuel Hood* (London, 1895).

The Marquis de Lafayette's papers are found in *Memoirs, Correspondence and Manuscripts of General Lafayette*, 3 vols. (London, 1837). There also are "Letters from Lafayette to Luzerne, 1780-1782," edited by Waldo G. Leland and Edmund C. Burnett, *American Historical Review* 20 (1914-1915).

For letters and documents pertaining to the southern campaigns see Robert W. Gibbes, ed., *Documentary History of the American Revolution*, 3 vols. (New York, 1853-1857).

Many of the French officers kept diaries and journals of their experiences in America during the revolution. Among the best of these are: Alexander Berthier, *Journal de la Campayne d'Amérique, 10 Mai, 1780 - 26 Août, 1781*, edited by Gilbert Chinard (Washington D.C., 1951); Edmond Pilon, ed., *Mémoires du Duc de Lauzan, General Biron*, (Paris, 1928); Claude Blanchard, *Guerre d'Amérique, 1780-1783* (Paris, 1881); Francois Jean, Marquis de Chastellux, *Travels in North America in the years 1780, 1781 and 1782*, edited by Howard C. Rice, Jr. (Chapel Hill, 1963); Samuel Green, ed., Comte Guillaume Des Deux-Ponts, *My Campaign in America: a Journal ... 1780-1781* (Boston, 1868); Lt. General Comte Mathieu Dumas, *Memoirs of His Own Time*, 2 vols. (Philadelphia, 1839); Hans Axel von Fersen, "Letters of Fersen, Written to His Father in Sweden, 1781-1782," *Magazine of American History* 3 (May-July, 1879); Francois Joseph Paul, Comte de Grasse, "Account of the Campaign of the Naval Armament under the Comte de Grasse," *Magazine of American History* 7 (1881); Jean-Baptiste-Donatien de Vimeur, Comte de Rochambeau, *Mémoires Militaries et Politique*, 2 vols. (Paris, 1829).

On the American side, the best journal covering the war was written by Dr. James Thatcher and published in Boston in 1827 under the title *A Military Journal during the American Revolutionary War*. Also see St. George Tucker, "The Southern Campaign, 1781—Narrated in the Letters from Judge St. George Tucker to his wife," *Magazine of American History* 7 (July, 1881).

A Hessian journal by Carl L. Baurmeister, entitled *Revolution in America* and edited by B.A. Uhlendorf (New Brunswick, 1957), conveys considerable light on events but should be used with caution since he sometimes wrote indiscriminately. Also of value is John Graves Simcoe's *A Military Journal* (New York, 1844).

Histories of the American Revolution appeared soon after the close of the war. The first was David Ramsay's *The History of the Revolution of South Carolina from British Province to an Independent State*, 2 vols. (Trenton, 1785). The next was by the British cavalry officer, Colonel Banastre Tarleton. His book, entitled *History of the Campaign of 1780 and 1781 in the Southern Provinces of North America* was published in Dublin in 1787. Following this there appeared a history by the Reverend William Gordon, who began compiling material for his work during the war. He was a frequent visitor at the American camps and knew Washington and many of the officers of the Continental army intimately. Gordon's work, which first appeared in four volumes, is entitled *History of the Rise, Progress and Establishment of the Independence of the United States of America* (London, 1788). Another history of the American Revolution appeared in 1789, when David Ramsay published his *History of the American Revolution*, 2 vols. (Philadelphia, 1789). An additional history by a British officer is Charles Stedman's *History of the Origins, Progress and Termination of the American War*, 2 vols. (London, 1794). In 1811, Henry Lee published a two-volume history entitled *Memoris of the War in the Southern Department of the United States* (Philadelphia, 1811). Like the others, it is written by a participant in the events, and contains important insights for the war in the South.

After the publication of the first histories of the American Revolution during the period following the war, writers leaned heavily upon these works and did not add much to the knowledge of the War of Independence for nearly a century. Finally, new interest in the American Revolution was generated by the centennial in 1876. Among the best was Henry P. Johnston's, *The Yorktown Campaign and the Surrender of Cornwallis* (New York, 1881).

The importance of the part played by navies during the American Revolution was highlighted by the publication of Alfred T. Mahan's *Major Operations of the Navies in the War of American Independence* (Boston, 1913). H.L. Landers *The Virginia Campaign and The Blockade and Siege of Yorktown, 1781* (Washington, D.C., 1931), also concentrated on the part exercised by the navies. Harold A. Larrabee's *Decision at the Chesapeake* (London, 1964), provides detail on eighteenth-century navies and the Battle of the Capes in September, 1781.

There are, of course, many biographies of Washington, beginning with John Marshall's *Life of George Washington*, 5 vols., (Philadelphia, 1804-1807). The most comprehensive biography of Washington is Douglas S. Freeman's *George Washington, a Biography*, 5 vols. (New York, 1948-1952), of which volume 3 covers the Yorktown campaign. A more recent biography is James T. Flexmen's *George Washington*, 3 vols. (Boston, 1965).

A scholarly treatment of Lord Cornwallis is found in Franklin and Mary Wickwire's *Cornwallis the American Adventure* (New York, 1970). Of exceptional value is William B. Willcox's *Portrait of a General: Sir Henry Clinton in the War of Independence* (New York, 1964). Unlike many other authors, Willcox does not condemn Clinton for his part in the Yorktown campaign. Since the strength of the French fleet was unknown to Clinton until after the Battle of the Capes, Willcox states that he had "compelling reasons for inaction."

In three volumes, George Washington Greene wrote a life of his grandfather General Nathanael Greene entitled *The Life of Nathanael Greene, Major-General in the Army of the Revolution* (New York, 1867-1871). This work contains extensive quotations from the letters of Nathanael Greene. A one-volume study of Greene is Theodore Thayer's *Nathanael Greene, Strategist of the American Revolution* (New York, 1960).

A scholarly biography of the Marquis de Lafayette by Charlemagne Tower, entitled *The Marquis de la Fayette in the American Revolution,* was published at Philadelphia in 1895. An excellent account of Lafayette's campaign in Virginia is to be found in Louis Gottschalk's *Lafayette and the Close of the American Revolution* (Chicago, 1942).

For General Knox's military career consult North Callahan's *Henry Knox, General Washington's General* (New York, 1958). The Battle of Cowpens is told by Don Higginbotham in *Daniel Morgan: Revolutionary Rifleman* (Chapel Hill, 1961), by North Callahan, *Daniel Morgan: Ranger of the Revolution* (New York, 1961), and by Burke Davis, *The Cowpens-Guilford Courthouse Campaign* (Philadelphia, 1960).

Concise sketches of the careers of Nathanael Greene, Horatio Gates, the Marquis de Lafayette and Daniel Morgan are in George Billias, ed., *George Washington's Generals* (New York, 1964). In *George Washington's Opponents,* also edited by Billias and published in 1967 are sketches of Sir Henry Clinton and Lord Cornwallis as well as of Admirals Mariott Arbuthnot, Thomas Graves, Samuel Hood, and George Rodney. None of the British admirals, however, have an adequate biographical treatment.

A life of Admiral de Grasse is Charles L. Lewis's, *Admiral De Grasse and American Independence* (Annapolis, 1945). The most recent biography of General Rochambeau is Arnold Whitridge, *Rochambeau: America's Neglected Founding Father* (New York, 1965).

Books on the Yorktown Campaign published in recent years are Burke Davis's *The Campaign That Won America: The Story of Yorktown* (New York, 1970), and Thomas J. Fleming's *Beat The Last Drum: The Siege of Yorktown, 1781* (New York, 1963). The books by Whitridge, Fleming, and Davis are popular in style.